FOCUS
Middle School
Economics

Mary C. Suiter, *Chair*

Joanne Dempsey

Mary Ann B. Pettit

Mary Lynn Reiser

National Council
on Economic Education

THE EconomicsAmerica AND EconomicsInternational PROGRAMS

990243

15311

AUTHORS

Mary C. Suiter, *Chair*
Associate Director, Center for Entrepreneurship and Economic Education, University of Missouri-St. Louis, St. Louis, Missouri

Joanne Dempsey
President, Illinois Council on Economic Education, Northern Illinois University, DeKalb, Illinois

Mary Ann B. Pettit
Associate Director, Center for Economic Education, Southern Illinois University-Edwardsville, Edwardsville, Illinois

Mary Lynn Reiser
Program Coordinator, Center for Economic Education, University of Nebraska-Omaha, Omaha, Nebraska

ACKNOWLEDGMENTS

The authors acknowledge the following teachers who field-tested and reviewed the lessons.

JoAnne Carlson
Lewis and Clark Junior High School
Omaha, Nebraska

Rich Clinch
Longfellow Middle School
Peoria, Illinois

Natalie Lynne Engelhardt
Norris Junior High School
Bellevue, Nebraska

Gayle Genovesi
Central Park School
Omaha, Nebraska

Dale R. Hoffman
Sterling Middle School
Peoria, Illinois

Susan M. Toohey
Lewis and Clark Junior High School
Omaha, Nebraska

Deborah Meyer
Blaine-Summer Middle School
Peoria, Illinois

Olivia Tallarico
Blaine-Summer Middle School
Peoria, Illinois

The authors acknowledge the following educators for reviewing the lessons.

Joan Sullivan Baranski
Former staff member
National Council on Economic Education

Patricia Elder
Vice President, EconomicsInternational
National Council on Economic Education

Martha Hopkins
Center for Economic Education
James Madison University

Sarapage McCorkle
Director
Center for Entrepreneurship and Economic Education
University of Missouri-St. Louis

Bonnie Meszaros
Associate Director
Center for Economic Education and Entrepreneurship
University of Delaware

Michael Watts
Director
Center for Economic Education
Purdue University

5 4 3 2

CONTENTS

FOREWORD   v

INTRODUCTION   vi
    Introductory Lesson: Economic Role Call   **vii**

UNIT 1: LIFELONG DECISION MAKER
    Introduction   **1**
    Lesson 1   The Path Not Taken   **2**
    Lesson 2   Give and Take   **9**

UNIT 2: KNOWLEDGEABLE CONSUMER
    Introduction   **15**
    Lesson 3   To Market, Which Market?   **16**
    Lesson 4   How Many Will You Buy?   **21**
    Lesson 5   Demand Shifters   **27**
    Lesson 6   Inflation   **34**

UNIT 3: PRODUCTIVE WORKER
    Introduction   **37**
    Lesson 7   The T-riffic T's Company: Production Decisions   **38**
    Lesson 8   How Many Should We Sell?   **46**
    Lesson 9   The Profit Puzzle   **58**

UNIT 4: RESPONSIBLE CITIZEN
    Introduction   **69**
    Lesson 10   Where Does the Money Go?   **70**
    Lesson 11   Where Does the Money Come From?   **79**
    Lesson 12   What Does the Nation Consume?   **88**
    Lesson 13   An Island Economy   **92**
    Lesson 14   No Free Lunch   **101**

UNIT 5: PRUDENT SAVER
    Introduction   **107**
    Lesson 15   Savers and Borrowers   **108**

UNIT 6: GLOBAL PARTICIPANT
    Introduction   **117**
    Lesson 16   Frontier Specialists   **118**
    Lesson 17   Don't Fence Me Out! (Barriers to Trade)   **125**

CONCLUDING LESSON: ROLE CALL QUIZ   137

GLOSSARY   149

BIBLIOGRAPHY   151

FOREWORD

Focus: Middle School Economics, a core volume in a new generation of National Council publications, is dedicated to increasing the economic literacy of *all* students. The *Focus* publications, the new centerpiece of EconomicsAmerica, build on almost five decades of success in delivering economic education to America's students.

The *Focus* series is both new and innovative, using economics primarily to enhance learning in subjects such as history, geography, civics, and personal finance. Activities are interactive, reflecting the belief that students learn best through active, highly personalized experiences with economics. Applications of economic understanding to real world situations and contexts dominate the lessons. In addition, the lessons explicitly teach the voluntary national standards in economics, outlined in the National Council's *A Framework for Teaching the Basic Economic Concepts*.

In *Focus: Middle School Economics*, the authors look at how social studies education can contribute to the development of effective participation in society. The focus in this publication is on six societal roles emphasized in

EconomicsAmerica: lifelong decision maker, knowledgeable consumer, productive worker, responsible citizen, prudent saver, and global participant. Middle school students may not yet perform all roles, but they will in the future. How they fill these roles will change as they grow and mature. The lessons emphasize that decision making is part of each of the societal roles that students will play, and students and teachers discover the economic content that is relevant to each role.

Michael Watts, Professor of Economics, Purdue University, and Senior Fellow, National Council on Economic Education, reviewed the manuscript and offered many valuable suggestions. The authors and the publisher are responsible for the final publication.

The National Council thanks the chief author, Mary Suiter, and other authors, Joanne Dempsey, Mary Ann Pettit, and Mary Lynn Rieser for their imaginative presentation of activities that help infuse economic content into social studies education in the middle school. We recognize, as well, the financial support of the National Science Foundation.

Robert F. Duvall, President & CEO
National Council on Economic Education

INTRODUCTION

OVERVIEW

The authors believe that social studies education in middle schools must focus on how people participate in society. Superka and Hawke, in an article in *Social Education*, state that, "If social education is to contribute more fully to the development of effective participants in our society, it must be refocused on how most people participate in that society—how they spend their time and where they put their energy." They further suggest that social studies education should focus on the roles common to members of society. The authors agree and, therefore, focus on six societal roles emphasized in EconomicsAmerica: lifelong decision maker, knowledgeable consumer, productive worker, responsible citizen, prudent saver, and global participant.

Middle school students may not yet perform all of the roles, but they will in the future. How they fill these roles will change as they grow and mature. The roles overlap in many ways. For example, decision making is part of each of the other roles, and prudent saver and global participant overlap with responsible citizen.

Focus: Middle School Economics includes an introduction, 19 lessons, a glossary, and a bibliography. The introduction includes a grid that correlates the lessons with related content areas and a grid that correlates the economic content with the lessons. An introductory lesson helps students understand the six roles emphasized in the program and the concept of an economic system.

Each unit has one of these six roles as a theme. The introduction to each unit focuses on the role featured in the unit and outlines the lessons in the unit. The lessons within each unit teach economic content relevant to a role students have or will have in the future. Each lesson has an introduction, a list of economic concepts, a list of related content areas, a set of objectives, a brief lesson description, an estimate of time required for the lesson, a list of materials required, procedure, closure, sug-gested evaluation, and list of extension activities that connect the lesson with other curricular content areas. In the last lesson of each unit, the evaluation section includes a journal writing activity to help students focus on their changing roles and the connection among roles by responding to the following questions:

- Is this one of your roles now? If so, how?
- How will you fill this role in the future?
- How will being a(n) _____(insert role)_____ benefit you?
- How is your role as decision maker related to being a(n) _____(insert role)_____?

The final lesson reviews the economics taught through a game and reviews the roles of individuals in the economic system. Also in the back matter are a glossary of economic terms and a bibliography listing fiction and nonfiction titles appropriate for teaching economics.

ABILITY GUIDELINES AND FLEXIBILITY OF TEXT

Focus: Middle School Economics is suitable for a wide variety of curriculum needs and teaching strategies. The program allows for great flexibility in teaching and learning—offering ample support for students of different ability levels. As there is no single approach or method adequate in all situations, the authors suggest many approaches for teachers to choose from to best suit the needs of their individual courses and to match the abilities, interests, and backgrounds of students. In general, the lessons are for all students.

KEY TO ABILITY LEVELS

The following coding system identifies activities suitable for students of various ability levels:

★ all students—basic course material
□ average and above average students
○ average and below average students

INTRODUCTORY LESSON

ECONOMIC ROLE CALL

INTRODUCTION

An economic system is the institutional framework that a society uses to allocate its resources to produce and distribute goods and services. In a predominantly market economic system, the major decisions about production and distribution are made in a decentralized manner by individual households and business firms.

As they participate in the economic system, members of society have a number of common roles: decision maker, consumer, worker, citizen, saver, and global participant. This lesson connects people's day-to-day activities to these roles and the economic system. Each of these six roles is a theme for a section of this publication. The lessons in each section will develop economic understanding related to the role.

ECONOMIC CONCEPTS

Economic system

RELATED CONTENT AREAS

Language arts
Critical thinking

OBJECTIVES

- ◆ Define economic system.
- ◆ Identify roles people have in the economy.
- ◆ Identify activities in which people engage that are related to their roles in the economy.
- ◆ Predict activities they will undertake in the future and relate them to the broad roles.

LESSON DESCRIPTION

Students participate in a game to identify six roles individuals have in our society. They learn that these roles are part of the economic system.

TIME REQUIRED

- ◆ Two class periods

MATERIALS

Dictionary
★Activity 1, *Economy Role Call*, one per student
★Activity 2, *Economy Role Call* Cards, cut apart
Chart paper
Markers

PROCEDURE

1. Explain that there are many things people do that are related to the roles they play in life. For example, teachers teach, shop, vote, pay taxes, and make choices in their roles as teachers, parents, and citizens.

2. Write **economic system** on the board. Ask students to suggest meanings for the term and/or to find the two words in the dictionary. Record their responses on the board. (Economic: related to the economy or money; the science that deals with the production, distribution, and consumption of commodities. System: a way of doing things; an organizational form; a group of interacting, interdependent elements forming a complex whole.)

3. Combine and develop students' responses into a definition such as this: An

---

★ all students—basic course material   □ average and above average students   ○ average and below average students

economic system is the framework that a society uses to allocate its resources to produce and distribute goods and services.

4. Explain that many things people do in their lives are related to the roles they have in the economic system.

5. Divide the class into groups and distribute Activity 1, *Economy Role Call*, to each student. Point out there are six sections on the page. Only a few letters are provided for each section heading.

6. Select a student to represent the role on *Economy Role Call* Card #1. Explain that there are three clues to help the class decide what role is being described. As the clues are announced, students write them under the corresponding section on the activity (for example, Section 1 for Card 1). Have students use the clues to determine the role and complete the section heading.

7. After the first role has been determined, ask the student with *Economy Role Call* Card #1 to write "Productive Worker" on the board and select a student to give the clues from *Role Call* Card # 2. Continue the process until all 6 roles have been determined. (**Note:** Upon completion there should be 6 columns on the board.)

8. After students have identified all of the roles, review the characteristics described by the clues. Discuss:

   • As a citizen, how does a person participate in the economy? (voting, paying taxes, obeying laws)

   • As a consumer, how does a person participate in the economy? (using and buying goods and services)

   • As a worker, how does a person participate in the economy? (helping to make goods or services in jobs or in their own households)

9. Ask students how someone participates

in the economy as a decision maker. (Answers will vary. Point out that being a decision maker is part of every role. People make decisions as workers, consumers, citizens, savers, and global participants.)

10. Ask students to think about activities related to one of the six roles. As students make suggestions, ask them to come forward and write them under the role to which the activity is related. (Student does homework: worker; student chooses how to spend allowance: consumer, decision maker; student has a savings account: saver; student obeys the laws of the community and the school: citizen; learns about other cultures, learns about rain forests: global participant.)

11. Ask students to predict activities they might perform as adults that are related to these roles. (Engineer: worker; tax payer, voter: citizen; bank customer: saver; becomes informed about a trade issue: global participant; chooses a college, job, car, and so on: decision maker.) As students answer, they write their suggestions in the correct column on the board.

CLOSURE

1. Have students construct a poster, write a poem, draw a picture, or in some creative way express the various roles they perform now or may perform in the future.

EVALUATION

1. Divide the class into groups of six. Distribute a sheet of chart paper to each group and a different colored marker to each student in the group. Instruct students to write their names on one side of the paper. On the other side, have them draw a circle in the center of the paper, write "economic system" inside the circle, and draw six lines out from the center circle. Next, they draw a circle at the end of each line and write one of the roles

inside each circle. Each student begins at one "role circle" writing ideas, words, and characteristics that suggest how this role is involved in the economic system. After two minutes, students move to the "role circle" on their left, look at the connections that have been made, and add some ideas of their own. Students continue moving every two minutes until each student has had a turn at each "role circle." Collect and keep the group webs. This activity can be conducted again in *Concluding Lesson, Role Call Quiz*, and the two webs can be compared for an evaluation. (Some possible connections: decision maker: voter, consumer; citizen: votes, pay taxes, uses public goods and services; consumer: buys goods, uses services.)

2. Instruct students to keep a journal for a week. Each day they enter activities of household members and identify the roles to which these activities are related.

EXTENSION

1. In their reading, ask students to identify ways characters in the books are involved in the economic system and to identify the roles to which the characters' activities might be related.

   Examples:
   Where the Red Fern Grows by Wilson Rawls (New York: Bantam, 1974): Billy and his parents work, save, and consume and in so doing make many decisions.

   The Great Wheel by Robert Lawson (New York: Walker, 1985): Conn Kilroy decides to leave his small village in Ireland for a new life in the United States. Conn's roles in the economic system include saver, citizen, worker, and decision maker.

2. In mathematics, ask students to solve problems related to consuming and saving (for example, calculating interest).

3. In social studies, introduce and review concepts related to the work and responsibilities of being a citizen.

4. Use *The International News Journal, Inc.* (New York: National Council on Economic Education, 1992), to expand student understanding of economics and student roles as global participants and productive workers.

5. Invite members of the community such as a government official or a childcare worker to speak to the class regarding their roles in the economy.

6. Divide the class into pairs of threes. Ask each group to write a script for a short play. Explain that the play must include examples of people participating in each of the six roles identified. Allow groups to

Name _____
ACTIVITY 1
ECONOMY ROLL CALL

1. _ _ R _ _ R

_____
_____
_____
_____
_____
_____

2. C _ N _ _ _ _ _ _

_____
_____
_____
_____
_____
_____

3. C _ _ _ Z _ _

_____
_____
_____
_____
_____

4. G L _ _ _ _ _
   P _ _ T I _ I P _ _ _

_____
_____
_____
_____
_____

5. _ _ V E _

_____
_____
_____
_____

6. D _ _ _ _ _ _ _ _
   M _ _ _ _

_____
_____
_____
_____
_____

ACTIVITY 2
ROLE CALL CLUE CARDS

1. WORKER a. Owns a business or works for someone else. b. Helps produce goods or services. c. Performs mental and/or physical work.	**2. CONSUMER** a. Decides what goods and services to buy. b. Spends money on goods and services. c. Uses goods and services.
3. CITIZEN a. Pays taxes. b. Obeys laws and acts responsibly. c. Becomes informed about issues and candidates and votes.	**4. GLOBAL PARTICIPANT** a. Tries to understand international trade issues. b. Learns about other cultures and civililzations. c. Seeks to understand the economics of environmental issues.
5. SAVER a. Gives up buying some goods and services now in order to buy goods and services in the future. b. Doesn't spend all of his or her income. c. Sometimes stores money in the bank and receives interest.	**6. DECISION MAKER** a. Determines his or her alternatives. b. Considers important factors about each alternative. c. Makes choices.

Correlations of Lessons with Related Content Area
(Including Extension Activities)

	Language Arts	Mathematics	Critical Thinking	Geography	History	Civics
Introduction	●	●	●			●
1	●		●		●	
2	●	●				
3	●	●		●		
4	●	●				
5	●	●				
6	●					
7	●	●	●			
8	●	●				
9	●	●				
10	●	●				●
11	●	●	●			●
12	●	●				●
13	●					●
14	●		●			●
15	●		●			
16	●	●			●	
17	●				●	
Concluding	●		●			●

ECONOMIC CONCEPT/LESSON GRID

CONCEPT	LESSON NUMBER									
	Intro	1	2	3	4	5	6	7	8	9
Scarcity		●						●		
Opportunity Cost and Trade-Offs		●	●							
Productivity								●		
Economic Systems	●									
Economic Institutions and Incentives										●
Exchange, Money, and Interdependence										
Markets and Prices				●	●					
Supply and Demand					●	●			●	
Competition and Market Structure										
Income Distribution										
Market Failures										
Role of Government										
Gross Domestic Product										
Unemployment										
Inflation							●			
Fiscal Policy										
Absolute and Comparative Advantage and Barriers to Trade										
Exchange Rates										
Tables								●		●
Charts and Graphs		●	●		●	●			●	
Ratios and Percentages			●							

ECONOMIC CONCEPT/LESSON GRID (continued)

CONCEPT	LESSON NUMBER								
	10	11	12	13	14	15	16	17	Concluding
Scarcity									
Opportunity Cost and Trade-Offs					●				
Productivity									
Economic Systems									●
Economic Institutions and Incentives						●			
Exchange, Money, and Interdependence							●		
Markets and Prices									
Supply and Demand									
Competition and Market Structure									
Income Distribution									
Market Failures	●								
Role of Government	●	●			●				
Gross Domestic Product			●	●					
Unemployment									
Inflation									
Fiscal Policy									
Absolute and Comparative Advantage and Barriers to Trade							●	●	
Exchange Rates									
Tables	●	●	●						
Charts and Graphs					●				
Ratios and Percentages	●	●	●						

INTRODUCTION TO LIFELONG DECISION MAKER

The two lessons in this unit introduce the economics related to the roles of individuals as decision makers. Decision making overlaps all roles students have and will have. Decision making is often a theme in the literature regarding adolescent students.

As they mature, students make decisions that can have dramatic impacts on their futures. Lessons in this unit help students practice decision-making skills both as individuals and in groups.

Lesson 1 introduces the concept of opportunity cost by asking students to consider decisions made by an entrepreneur, Madam C. J. Walker, and the opportunity costs of her decisions.

Lesson 2 helps students recognize the trade-offs that result when choices are made.

THE PATH NOT TAKEN

INTRODUCTION

Throughout history, entrepreneurs have assumed the risk of organizing natural, human, and capital resources to produce goods and services. In doing so, entrepreneurs make choices and incur opportunity costs. Opportunity cost is the highest valued alternative that must be forgone because another option is chosen.

ECONOMIC CONCEPTS

Choices
Alternatives
Entrepreneur
Opportunity cost

RELATED CONTENT AREAS

Language arts (flowcharts)

OBJECTIVES

◆ Identify choices.
◆ Define opportunity cost.
◆ Define entrepreneur.

LESSON DESCRIPTION

Students create a decision/opportunity cost flowchart for *Madam C. J. Walker.*

TIME REQUIRED

◆ Two class periods

MATERIALS

Transparency Visual 1, *Joe's Flowchart*
Dictionary
★ Activity 1, *Madam C. J. Walker: The Path Not Taken* for each student
Transparency of Visual 2, *Madam C. J. Walker Flowchart*
Literature or social studies books
Highlight markers or ink pens

PROCEDURE

1. Discuss a choice made in the past week. Ask students to talk about choices they have made during that week. Record these choices on one side of an overhead transparency or on the chalkboard.

2. Ask students to identify the alternative they passed up. For example, if someone chose to attend a soccer game after school, what did he or she give up the opportunity to do in that same period of time? (Answers will vary.)

3. Explain that this forgone option is called an **opportunity cost**. Opportunity cost is the highest valued alternative that must be given up when another option is chosen.

4. Discuss other choices made by individuals, groups, schools, and governments using local examples wherever possible. Identify the opportunity cost associated with each of these choices. Remember to emphasize that opportunity cost is not all other possible alternatives but rather the single highest valued alternative not taken.

5. Display Visual 1, *"Joe's Flowchart,"* and explain that people make many choices each day. The flowchart shows examples of two choices Joe made this morning and the opportunity cost of each of those choices.

   • Joe had to choose between sleeping longer or getting up when his alarm went off. He chose to get up. What was his opportunity cost? (sleeping longer) Shade "sleeping longer" with the overhead pen.

   • Joe got up on time so he had time to eat breakfast. He chose to eat a bagel. What was his opportunity cost? (cereal) Shade "cereal" with overhead pen.

   • Joe had to choose between a sweatshirt or a T-shirt this morning. He chose the T-shirt. What was his opportunity cost? (sweatshirt) Shade "sweatshirt" with the overhead pen.

6. Explain that a flowchart uses geometric figures and arrows to depict graphically possible and actual events. Flowcharts are often used to simplify complex ideas. Tell students they will use flowcharts to illustrate decision making and opportunity cost.

7. Instruct students to list several decisions they made yesterday after getting home from school. (What to eat, whether to do homework or watch television, and so on.)

8. Allow students time to create their own decision flowcharts using their lists of after-school decisions. Have them underline the opportunity cost of each decision.

9. Write the word entrepreneur on the board. Ask students to use the dictionary to find the origin of the word. (Entrepreneur, from the French word entreprendre, meaning to undertake.)

10. Explain that entrepreneurs "undertake" or assume the risk of organizing natural, human, and capital resources to produce goods and services. Entrepreneurship involves more than being in business or owning a business. Entrepreneurs are creative, resourceful, and innovative.

11. Ask students for examples of times they have been creative, resourceful, innovative, or of a time they have undertaken risk.

12. Provide examples and ask students to provide examples of entrepreneurs. (Andrew Carnegie, steel; James S. McDonnell, aircraft, space; Joseph Pulitzer, newspapers; Milton Bradley, games; Jan Matzlinger, shoes; Ray Kroc, McDonald's; Berry Gordy, Jr., Motown; Mrs. Fields, cookies; Dave Thomas, Wendy's.)

13. Explain that entrepreneurs make decisions and incur opportunity costs. When entrepreneurs use their time to develop and operate their own ventures (businesses), they give up alternative uses for their time. When they decide to use their money for one project, they give up being able to use it for another project.

14. Distribute a highlight marker or pen and a copy of Activity 1 to each student.

15. Have students read the biographical sketch and highlight or underline the choices Madam C. J. Walker made during her life. After highlighting these choices, students make lists of these choices and next to each choice write what they think her opportunity cost was. Emphasize that answers will vary and that there are many possibilities.

16. Discuss some of the choices and opportunity costs students noted.

    Choice
    • married a carpenter
    • worked as a washerwoman
    • moved to St. Louis
    • saved money

    Opportunity Cost
    • gave up being single
    • gave up staying at home
    • gave up home and job in Vicksburg
    • gave up spending money

17. Display Visual 2, illustrating a flowchart of Madam C. J.'s life up through her move to St. Louis.

18. Have students complete a flowchart of Madam C. J. Walker's life using whatever symbols they wish. For each of her choices, students shade or color in her opportunity cost.

19. After students complete their flowchart discuss:
    • Why was Madam C. J. Walker an example of an entrepreneur? (She organized resources to produce a

good. She was creative, resourceful, and innovative. She undertook risk.)

- What problem was she attempting to solve? (How to restore hair growth.)

- What risks did she take in starting and operating her business? (Moving to Denver without a certain job; trying to find work in Denver; attempting to perfect her products.)

- In what ways was she creative? (Adding sulfur to her tonics, developing several tonics, using door-to-door sales.)

- In what ways was she resourceful? (Working and saving money while perfecting her product; listening to and learning from others; recognizing and taking advantage of new opportunities.)

- In what ways was she innovative? (Placing her products on the market, organizing and training a door-to-door sales force.)

- How might Madam Walker's life been different if she had made different choices? (Answers will vary.)

CLOSURE

1. Review the following.

   - People make choices every day.

   - When choices are made, something is given up.

   - The highest forgone alternative is the opportunity cost.

   - Entrepreneurs undertake or assume the risk of organizing natural, human, and capital resources to produce goods and services.

   - Entrepreneurs make decisions and face opportunity costs.

   - Entrepreneurs are innovative, creative, and resourceful.

EVALUATION

1. Select short biographies from the class literature or social studies books or ask stu-

dents to do some research about entrepreneurs. Instruct students to prepare a flowchart of the person's life, portraying choices made and identifying opportunity costs. Students should also identify examples of innovative, resourceful, or creative behaviors.

2. Ask students to select well-known athletes, musicians, or other public figures and identify choices and opportunity costs in their lives.

3. Have students ask adults to identify choices and opportunity costs in their lives.

EXTENSION

1. Use Lessons 1, 2, 3, and 4 from Unit 1, *Entrepreneurship in the U.S. Economy*, (New York: National Council on Economic Education, 1994).

2. Invite local entrepreneurs to speak to the class. Ask them to describe some of the choices they made and the alternatives forgone.

3. Instruct pairs of students to interview the principal, teachers, and staff members regarding choices they have made and alternatives forgone. Using the interview information, instruct students to develop headlines and articles for an "opportunity cost" newspaper.

4. As a class, read *The Store That Mama Built* by Robert Lehrman (New York: Macmillan, 1992), or the biography of an entrepreneur. Ask students to keep a journal. Journal entries could include:

   - In what ways did the character(s) demonstrate creativity? Resourcefulness? The ability to be innovative?

   - What education, training, skills, and abilities did the character(s) possess?

   - What problem was the character(s) attempting to solve or what want was he or she attempting to satisfy?

- What risks did the character(s) take in attempting to solve a problem or satisfy a want?
- What choices did the character(s) make? What were the opportunity costs of these choices?

- Did the character(s) undertake endeavors that failed? If so, how did he or she handle failure?
- Did the character(s) recognize and take advantage of new opportunities?

VISUAL 1
JOE'S FLOWCHART

Joe's Morning

| Sleep later | Get up when alarm goes off | Wear T-shirt | Wear sweatshirt |

| Skip breakfast | Eat breakfast |

| Cereal | Bagel |

VISUAL 2
MADAM C. J. WALKER
FLOWCHART
SAMPLE

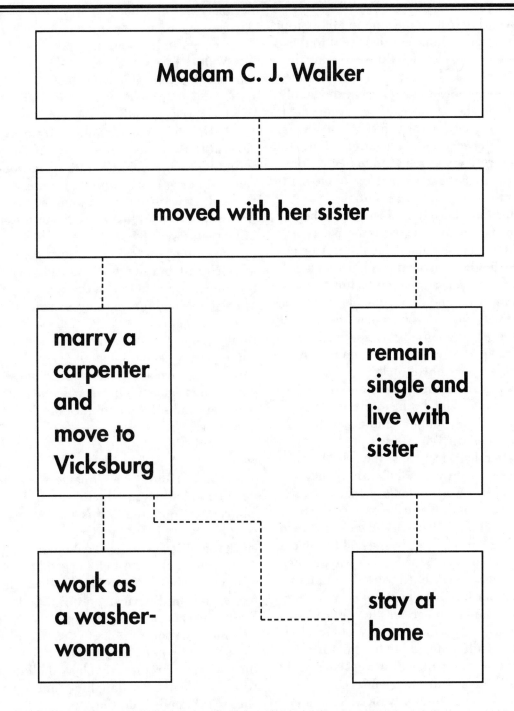

Name _____

ACTIVITY 1
THE PATH NOT TAKEN: MADAM C. J. WALKER

Sarah Breedlove was born in 1867, two years after the end of the Civil War. Her parents were freed slaves who worked the land in Mississippi as sharecroppers. They paid their rent to the landowner in crops, leaving little extra for the family. At a very early age Sarah and her older sister took in laundry to supplement the family income. When she was seven, her parents died of yellow fever, leaving the two sisters orphans. When her sister married, Sarah went along, but her brother-in-law was not kind to her. At the age of 14 she married a carpenter and moved to Vicksburg to escape the bad situation.

She helped her husband, Moses McWilliams support the family by working as a washerwoman. At age 17, she had a daughter, A'Lelia. Soon after that her husband was killed in an accident. Sarah learned that opportunities existed in the West and decided to move with her daughter to St. Louis to start a new life. She was able to get work as a laundress and was determined to make a better life for her daughter.

Sarah was a very hard worker and saved enough money for an apartment and for A'Lelia to attend school. She even saved enough to send A'Lelia to a small African-American college in Tennessee.

Sarah attended a lecture at the 1904 World's Fair given by Mrs. Booker T. Washington. Sarah took Mrs. Washington's lecture to heart. After years of concentrating her energies on raising a daughter, Sarah was inspired to begin improving her own life. First she had to solve a personal problem that stood in her way. Either from poor diet or very hard work, Sarah had lost most of her hair. She began experimenting with various tonics and creams to restore hair. She had a dream in which she was told to order a compound (sulfur) to add to her mixture. Amazingly the tonic with sulfur worked and she began to sell the mixture to friends. One of her friends was Charles Joseph Walker, a newspaper salesman. Mr. Walker gave her some excellent advice about selling her product.

Sarah decided it would be good to sell her product in an area where she had less competition and a stronger market. With $1.50 in savings, she moved to Denver to make her fortune. She worked as a cook for a wealthy pharmacist and saved her money while perfecting her three main products, Wonderful Hair Grower, Glossine, and Vegetable Shampoo. These products became extremely popular within Denver's African-American community. While living in Denver, Sarah had kept up her friendship with Mr. Walker by mail. Finally, they were married and Sarah renamed her product line "Madam C. J. Walker" to add an air of mystery. Her products were the talk of Denver.

Charles thought she should concentrate her sales in Denver but Madam Walker had a different idea. She embarked on a year and a half sales trip across the country training a sales force of African-American women to distribute her product. Sales boomed. Because so many of her sales were by mail, she decided to move her headquarters to a more central city. She selected Pittsburgh. In Pittsburgh, her daughter joined her to help run the company. They opened a school for training Walker sales women called Lelia College. This was a revolutionary concept for training and is still widely copied today. The women all dressed in black skirts and starched white blouses and were very well groomed. They learned about the products and sales techniques for door-to-door sales.

In 1911, the sales force had grown to 950 women. The business grew so fast that it outgrew the Pittsburgh headquarters, so she decided to build a new factory in Indianapolis. Charles was opposed to this expansion and the couple divorced. Madam C. J. Walker expanded the sales force to the Caribbean and Central American markets. A'Lelia urged her mother to move the headquarters to Harlem, the center of African-American culture. Madam C. J. Walker became a celebrity and was invited by President Wilson to come to the White House. In 1918, Madam C. J. Walker officially became the country's first female black millionaire. After her death, her daughter continued the successful family tradition.

GIVE AND TAKE

INTRODUCTION

Often decisions result in trading off some of one thing to get some of another. This lesson introduces the idea of trade-offs and provides practice in analyzing options before making decisions.

ECONOMIC CONCEPTS

Choice
Opportunity cost
Alternatives
Trade-offs

RELATED CONTENT AREAS

Mathematics
Charts and graphs
Use of calculators

OBJECTIVES

◆ Define opportunity cost.

◆ Identify alternatives.

◆ Explain that a trade-off involves giving up some of one thing to get some of another.

◆ Analyze trade-offs.

LESSON DESCRIPTION

After reading about a problem, students identify alternative solutions, trade-offs made in choosing each alternative, and the opportunity cost of selecting each option. Students describe trade-offs and create a graphic to represent alternatives and trade-offs.

TIME REQUIRED

◆ Two class periods

MATERIALS

Visual 1, *Basketball Dilemma*, and 2, *Basketball Options*
Calculator for every 2–3 students
Overhead pens
Markers for each group
★ Activity 1, *Options*, for each student
Newspaper ads for food and other items

PROCEDURE

1. Explain that sometimes decisions result in giving up some of one thing to get some of another thing. This is called a **trade-off.**

2. Display transparency of Visual 1 and ask students to identify the problem in this situation. (The main gym is available only for 8 hours but the students will play 20 basketball games.) Explain there are two obvious choices. The students could use all 8 hours for girls' games or all 8 hours for boys' games.

3. Ask students to identify other options. List these on the board. (4 hours for girls, 4 hours for boys; 6 hours for girls; 2 hours for boys, 6 hours for boys, 2 hours for girls; 3 hours for boys, 5 hours for girls; 3 hours for girls, 5 hours for boys; and so on.) Select a student and discuss:

   • If you were making this decision, what option would you choose? (Answers will vary but use one student's answer as an example.)

   • What would your second choice be? What do we call this second choice? (opportunity cost)

   • Does choosing this option result in any trade-offs? (Yes, you give up being able to play some boys' (girls') games in order to play some girls' (boys') games.)

4. Display transparency of Visual 2. Discuss sample charts and keys. Using the blank box on the transparency, demonstrate another option.

5. Divide the class into groups of 2–3 students. Distribute calculators and markers to each group. Ask students to illustrate as many options as they can and determine the percent of time in the large gym allotted to each group. They may use squares, circles, or rectangles.

6. Distribute a copy of Activity 1 to each student. Assign each group one of the situations on the sheet. Instruct the group to determine a list of possible options, and assign time or money values.

7. Ask students to use the back side of Activity 1 to draw pie charts or graphs representing each option they have described. Instruct them to identify the choice they would make, their opportunity cost, and the trade-offs resulting from their decision.

CLOSURE

1. Ask groups to tell which situation they were assigned, identify options they listed, their decision and opportunity cost, and the trade-offs that resulted.

EVALUATION

1. Instruct groups to write their own decision situations that have a variety of possible outcomes. When paragraphs are complete, have them trade with another group, calculate percentages, and develop a graph. Explain that depending on the options, they may wish to use something other than a pie chart.

2. Ask students to answer the following questions in their *Economics Role Journal* regarding the role of lifelong decision maker.
   - Is this one of your roles now? If so, how?
   - How will you fill this role in the future?
   - How will being a good decision maker benefit you?

EXTENSION

1. Ask students to look for pie charts in news magazines and newspapers. Instruct them to translate one of their decision graphs into another visual format (such as a bar graph).

2. Instruct students to collect pictures or headlines from newspapers that describe local economic decisions. Students identify the trade-offs in these decisions and develop a presentation that identifies the pros and cons of each alternative and the decision/trade-off involved. They may use visuals in their presentations.

VISUAL 1
BASKETBALL DILEMMA

Latoya and Jeff were asked by their basketball coaches to help schedule the intramural tournament at their middle school. The school has two gyms in which games can be played but only the main gym has bleachers and a concession stand.

The girls will play 9 games and the boys will play 11 games. The games are 50 minutes long with a 10 minute break between games. The main gym is available for 8 hours. The other, smaller gym will be used for the remaining games.

The coaches asked Latoya and Jeff to list as many scheduling options as possible for the large gym. List as many options as you can for scheduling the main gym.

VISUAL 1
BASKETBALL OPTIONS

Large Gym

♀♀♀♀♀ ♂♂♂♂♂
♀♀♀♀♀ ♂♂♂♂♂
♀♀♀♀♀ ♂♂♂♂♂
♀♀♀♀♀ ♂♂♂♂♂

Key:

♀♀♀♀♀ **girls' game**

♂♂♂♂♂ **boys' game**

4 hours = $1/2$ = 50% for boys' games
4 hours = $1/2$ = 50% for girl's games

♀♀♀♀♀ ♂♂♂♂♂
♀♀♀♀♀ ♂♂♂♂♂

♀♀♀♀♀ ♂♂♂♂♂
♀♀♀♀♀ ♂♂♂♂♂

2 hours = $1/4$ = 25 % for boy's games
6 hours = $3/4$ = 75 % for girls' games

 From *Focus: Middle School Economics*, © National Council on Economic Education, New York, NY

Name _____

ACTIVITY 1
OPTIONS

Analyze the following situations and list the options available to the individuals involved. When necessary, make up an exact number of hours or dollar amounts to fit the situation. (For example, cost of food or other items, amount of space, hours of time.) Based on your numbers, calculate the percentages for each option.

1. Maria received $15 from her aunt for her birthday and decided to go to the mall to look over her choices. After visiting several stores, she has decided she could purchase a CD of her favorite band, candy from the jellybean store, new pens and markers, or food from the food court. Use newspaper ads as well as your own experience to assign prices to these items and determine Maria's options.

2. Doug planned to go skate boarding this afternoon with his friend Rick at 1:00. He has to be home to help his mother prepare dinner at 5:00. An hour ago, he was asked to mow the neighbor's lawn. The neighbor will pay extra if Doug will do the job this afternoon. What are Doug's options?

3. Sheena is trying out for the basketball team at school. She has to be able to make free throws and three-point shots. She has three hours to practice this afternoon. How much time should she spend practicing each skill? What are her options?

4. Randy and Larry are in charge of the refreshments for the party after the class play. Their budget for snack food is $20. They are considering popcorn, pretzels, chips, nuts, and nachos. Use newspaper ads and your own experience to assign prices to these items. What are their options?

5. Luis has an English final tomorrow and has only two hours to study this evening. He knows that spelling words will be on the final but he also knows there will be questions covering the rules of grammar and punctuation. How could he plan his study time?

6. Sally is attending a scout camp in the mountains for a week. The campers will be hiking, camping, and horseback riding. They also have certain jobs they must do each day and special projects they must complete. They have only two hours during each of four days to schedule hiking, camping, and horseback riding. Each activity must be scheduled in 30 minute blocks. Sally wants to spend some time doing each of these activities. What are her options?

INTRODUCTION TO KNOWLEDGEABLE CONSUMER

From an early age, students participate in the economy as consumers. The four lessons in this section provide students with information about markets and consumer behavior to assist them in their roles as consumers and decision makers.

Lesson 3 introduces the concept of market and the conditions necessary for a market to exist. Students identify markets in their communities and the criteria they use for purchasing goods and services in a particular market.

Lesson 4 establishes a demand schedule and the relationship between price and quantity demanded.

Lesson 5 gives students the opportunity to study the nonprice determinants of demand and their effect on the demand for products.

In Lesson 6, students learn about inflation and the impact of inflation on their purchasing power.

TO MARKET, WHICH MARKET?

INTRODUCTION

A market exists whenever buyers and sellers exchange goods and services. Markets have existed throughout history. Students are participants in many markets.

ECONOMIC CONCEPTS

Market
Goods
Services
Exchange

RELATED CONTENT AREAS

Language arts (chart, surveys)
Geography (place–location)

OBJECTIVES

◆ Recognize markets as places where buyers and sellers exchange goods and services.

◆ Identify themselves as consumers of goods and services.

◆ List areas in their community that serve as markets.

◆ Analyze why markets in their communities are successful or unsuccessful.

LESSON DESCRIPTION

In this lesson, students consider how markets have changed throughout history, describe the markets where they exchange goods and services, and predict new markets that may develop.

TIME REQUIRED

◆ One class period

MATERIALS

○ Activity 1, *The Modern-Day Market*, for each group

○ Visual 1, *Market Quiz*
○ Activity 2, *Why Do You Buy Where You Buy*, for each student

PROCEDURE

1. Ask students what comes to mind when they hear the word "market" in the nursery rhyme, "To market, to market to buy a fat pig; home again, home again, jiggity jig."

2. As a class, generate a list of markets that have occurred throughout history (students may need reference books for this). Write the list on the board or an overhead. The list might include, Greek agoras, early markets of Rome and China, the Cardo of Jerusalem, medieval fairs, colonial markets and seaports, and caravans. Discuss the differences and similarities of these markets. (Differences: location, types of goods available, method of exchange; similarities: buyers, sellers, products, exchange taking place.)

3. Explain that the similarities define any market. A **market** exists whenever buyers and sellers exchange goods and services. Review the terms goods and services by asking students for examples of goods and services they purchased in the past 24 hours. Make sure that the goods are tangible items and the services are things people do for others.

4. Divide the class into groups of 3–4. Distribute a copy of Activity 1 to each group. Discuss each example briefly.

5. Display transparency of Visual 1. Explain that there are many businesses in a community. These businesses make up the market for goods and services in the community. The businesses are located in a variety of places, for example, malls, strip malls, downtown business sections, catalog services, and so on. All of these businesses provide goods and/or services. Ask students to complete Activity 1 by answering the questions on the transparency for five of the businesses/locations listed. Then ask students to draw

★ all students—basic course material   □ average and above average students   ○ average and below average students

generalizations about the similarities and differences regarding these businesses/locations.

6. Distribute a copy of Activity 2 to each student. Instruct them to work in pairs and fill in the first blank column, listing local businesses where their families buy goods and services.

7. Ask pairs of students to report their lists. After students have reported, discuss:
   - Are some items bought in more than one type of business? (yes)
   - Why do some people choose one business over another (for example, catalog over discount store)? (Answers will vary.)

CLOSURE

1. Tell pairs of students to discuss the reasons why their families shop in particular businesses and list the primary reason in the appropriate column on Activity 2. Reasons could include convenience, location, loyalty to owner, atmosphere, prices, image of shoppers, readily available parking, very high quality merchandise or service, and so on.

2. Ask pairs of students to report the primary reasons they have listed for choosing a business. As they report, list their answers on the board. If a group gives a reason that has already been listed, place a check mark next to the reason to tally the number of groups that listed it.

3. Explain that the list on the board represents criteria consumers use in making decisions about where to buy various goods and services.

4. Ask students to think of a business that has recently failed in their community. Ask if failure of the business could be linked to any of the criteria listed on the board. For example, the business might have been a restaurant in an inconvenient location; the prices might have been

too high relative to other similar restaurants; and so on.

EVALUATION

1. Write some of the answers students gave in column 2 of Activity 2 (name of business) on slips of paper. Place the slips of paper in a container. Ask each student to draw one of the slips and write a statement explaining why the business listed is part of the market for goods and services. (It is a place/way that buyers and sellers come together, exchange takes place, goods and/or services are available.)

2. Tell students to write a paragraph explaining why someone would choose one business over another when purchasing a good.

3. Divide the class into small groups and instruct them to think of goods and services consumers will want in the future and the ways in which these goods and services will be provided.

EXTENSION

1. Instruct students to select an ad from the local paper and write a paragraph analyzing the appeal a business has for consumers based on the criteria list the class developed. (For example, price, location, brand names.)

2. Place a map of the community on a bulletin board with the heading *Businesses in Our Community*. Allow students to make "business flag" push pins. Instruct them to locate the various places they listed in Activity 1 on the map and place a "business flag" pin there.

3. Develop a consumer criteria survey list using the criteria the class listed in Activity 2. Instruct each student to ask three students from other classes to rank the criteria on the survey in order of importance. Combine the information students collect and develop a criteria bar graph to complement the map bulletin board.

ACTIVITY 1
THE MODERN-DAY MARKET

		Name	Some Goods & Services Provided	How Do They Attract Consumers?	Hours Open	How Do People Interact?
1.	Regional Mall					
2.	Strip Mall					
3.	Downtown Business District					
4.	Catalog					
5.	Home Shopping Channel					
6.	Want Ads					
7.	Auto Mall					
8.	Computer Shopping Line					

VISUAL 1
MARKET QUIZ

Select five locations listed on the *The Modern-Day Market* activity and answer the following questions about each of the five.

1. Name one of these businesses/locations in your local community.

2. Name some goods and services it provides.

3. How are consumers attracted to this business/location?

4. What hours is it open?

5. How do buyers and sellers interact?

Name _____
ACTIVITY 2
WHY DO YOU BUY WHERE YOU BUY?

Every day you and your family make decisions about consuming goods services. You make purchases at many different businesses in your own community. Listed below are products and services that you or your family might use. List the name of a business in your community where you have bought the good or service.

Good or Service	Business Where Family Buys This Good or Service	Primary Reason Family Buys Here
1. Fresh fruits or vegetables		
2. Blue jeans		
3. Sunday newspaper		
4. Gasoline		
5. Auto repair		
6. Fried chicken or pizza		
7. Haircut		
8. Movie rental		
9. Clothes cleaning		
10. Booster shot/vaccination		

HOW MANY WILL YOU BUY?

INTRODUCTION

Consumers buy products every day in various markets around the world. Retailers and manufacturers are interested in consumer behavior because they want to produce products that will be popular with consumers, deliver the products to markets, and sell the products for a profit. Understanding consumer behavior includes understanding demand. As the price of a product decreases, the quantity consumers buy goes up. This inverse relationship is called the Law of Demand. Economists define demand as the relationship between various prices and the quantities consumers are willing and able to buy during some time period, holding all other factors constant.

ECONOMIC CONCEPTS

Price
Quantity demanded
Demand

RELATED CONTENT AREAS

Mathematics (graphs)
Language arts

OBJECTIVES

◆ Describe the relationship between price and quantities demanded.

◆ Construct a demand schedule for a product.

◆ Analyze reasons for the inverse relationship between price and quantity demanded.

◆ Survey a group to determine their willingness to purchase a product.

◆ Define demand.

LESSON DESCRIPTION

In this lesson students participate in an activity to establish a demand schedule for a product. They discuss the relationship between price and quantity, graph demand, and conduct a market survey.

TIME REQUIRED

◆ Two class periods

MATERIALS

Newspaper headline (see Procedure Step 1)
Visual 1, *How Many Will We Buy?* and
     Visual 2, *Demand Graph*
☐ Activity 1, *Demand Graph*

PROCEDURE

1. Find a local newspaper headline about the closing of a local business to use as a discussion starter. If one is not available, write the following headline on the board: "Drop in Demand Forces Local Hardware Store to Close." Ask students what comes to mind when they read the headline.

2. Explain that one segment of economics involves analyzing consumer behavior. This includes consumer demand for goods and services. Remind students that consumers use goods and services.

3. Write the names of four types of beverages across the top of the blackboard or tape signs with a beverage name written on each in four areas of the classroom. (Cola, Fruit Juice, Sparkling Water, Milk.)

4. Explain that each student has a budget of $3.00 and can buy **one** 12-ounce container of a beverage. Explain that the price is $1.00. Instruct them to stand beneath the heading or sign for the beverage they want to buy. Ask students to indicate how many containers they would buy.

5. Select the beverage most frequently chosen. This will be the beverage for which you will develop a demand schedule.

★ all students—basic course material   ☐ average and above average students   ○ average and below average students   **21**

6. Display transparency of Visual 1. Across from $1.00 in the price column record the number of containers students would buy.

7. Announce that the price of the other beverages is still $1.00 but the price of the most popular beverage is now $1.50. Ask if any students would like to change their minds. If so, allow them to move to another beverage area.

8. Count the number of containers students in the most popular beverage area would buy. Next to $1.50 record the quantity demanded on the transparency.

9. Repeat steps 7 and 8 for a price of $2.00 and $2.50 for the same beverage.

10. Have students return to their seats and look at the table on the transparency. Ask what they can conclude about consumer behavior and the price of a product. (As the price goes down, the quantity consumers are willing and able to buy goes up. As price goes up, the quantity consumers are willing and able to buy goes down.)

11. Explain that this inverse relationship between price and quantity demanded is called the **Law of Demand**.

12. Ask students why they think consumers are willing and able to buy more of a product at a lower price. (With a given amount of income, a lower price means consumers can afford to buy more of a product and when the price of a product falls, consumers will substitute this less expensive product for more expensive similar products.)

13. Refer back to the transparency. Explain that a single price in the table corresponds to a specific quantity demanded; however, the various prices and quantities together make up the class **demand** for the beverage.

14. Write the word **Demand** above the table on the transparency.

15. Explain that demand is the relationship between various prices and the quantities consumers are willing and able to buy during some time period, all other things being equal. The only thing that changes during the time period is the price of the product.

16. Distribute a copy of Activity 1 to each student. Instruct students to write the beverage name in the blank and record the information from the transparency above the graph.

17. Display transparency of Visual 2. Explain that demand may also be illustrated graphically. When graphing demand, price is recorded on the vertical axis and quantity on the horizontal axis. Instruct students to label the vertical axis *Price* and the horizontal axis *Quantity* as you label the transparency.

18. As a class, scale each axis and plot the first point ($1.00 and the quantity demanded at $1.00). Instruct students to plot the 3 remaining points and connect the points, creating a demand curve.

CLOSURE

1. Use the following questions to discuss the graph:
   - What does the graph represent? (The class demand for selected beverage.)
   - What does the curve look like? (It is downward sloping; it slopes down and to the right.)
   - Why is the curve downward sloping? (Because as the price of the product goes down, the quantity demanded goes up and vice versa.)
   - What kind of relationship is this? (inverse)
   - What do we call this inverse relationship? (The law of demand.)
   - Which picture of demand is easier to understand, the table or the graph? (Answers will vary.)

EVALUATION

1. Decide on a product the class could sell (bookmark, stationery, popcorn). Write a brief description of the product that could be used in an advertisement. Establish several possible prices for a unit of the product. Instruct students to conduct a market survey by interviewing one or more household members regarding the quantities they would purchase at the various prices. As a class, compile all the data to complete a product demand schedule. Ask students to plot the demand schedule data to illustrate the demand for the product.

2. Have students write a paragraph describing a time when a change in price affected their buying decisions. (For example, the price went up and they bought less of something, or the price went down and they bought more of something.)

EXTENSION

1. Have students collect ads from the local newspaper for a product. Using the prices found in the ads and pictures from the ads or pictures students draw, instruct them to create a visual representing the law of demand.

2. Ask students to brainstorm things, other than price, that influence what they buy. (Examples may include: number of consumers, tastes and preferences, income price of related goods.)

3. Use Lesson 5, *Demand Shifters* from this unit, to introduce the non-price determinants of demand.

4. Use the *International News Journal, Inc.*, (New York: National Council on Economic Education, 1992). (Students conduct a market survey.)

5. Read *Homer Price (The Doughnuts)* by Robert McCloskey (New York: Puffin Books, 1964), and use the corresponding lesson in *Economics and Children's Literature* (SPEC Publishers, Inc., St. Louis, MO, 1993).

VISUAL 1
HOW MANY WILL WE BUY?

Price	Quantity Demanded
$ 2.50	
2.00	
1.50	
1.00	

Name _____
ACTIVITY 1
Demand for _____

Using the graph below, illustrate the demand schedule for the product. Price is plotted on the vertical axis and Quantity Demanded on the horizontal axis. Label the bottom left-hand corner as 0.

Price	Quantity Demanded
$2.50	
2.00	
1.50	
1.00	

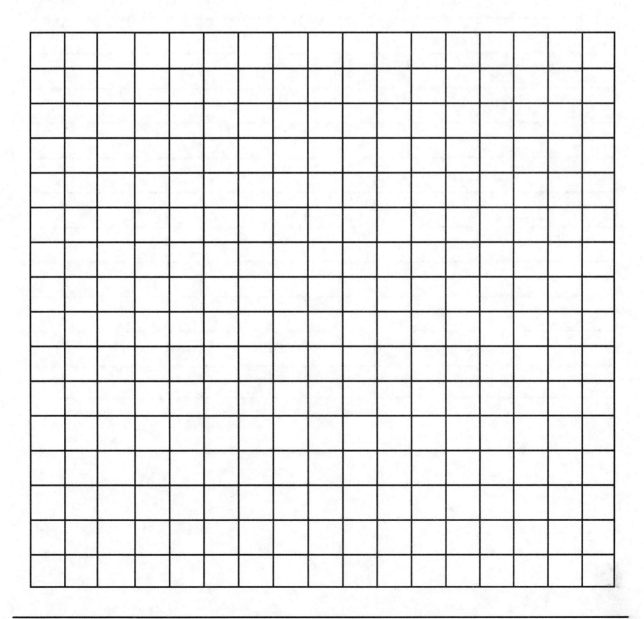

VISUAL 2
DEMAND GRAPH

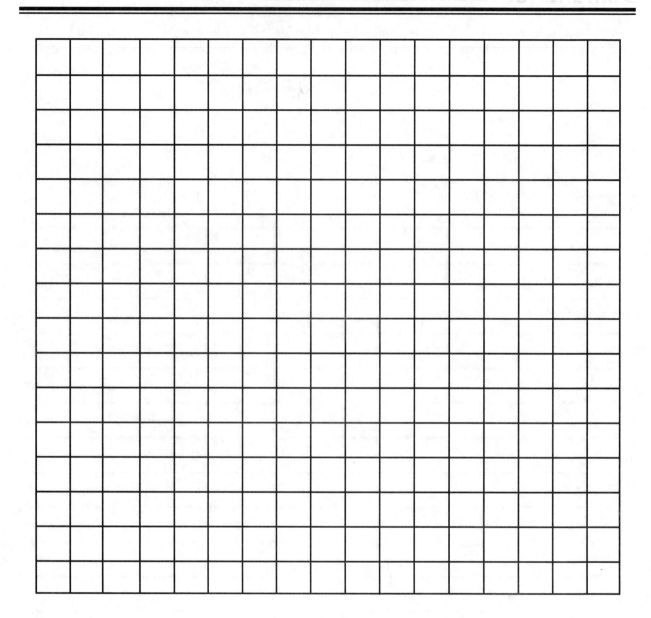

DEMAND SHIFTERS

INTRODUCTION

This lesson is a companion to Lesson 4, *How Many Will You Buy?* and should be used following that lesson.

Adolescents as a group play an important part in total consumer spending. For this reason, it is important that they learn to analyze their spending habits and recognize factors that influence their behavior. This lesson reviews the law of demand, demand, and quantity demanded and introduces the nonprice determinants of demand. These are the factors held constant when establishing the demand for a product. They include: number of consumers in the market, consumer tastes and preferences, consumer income, and prices of related goods.

ECONOMIC CONCEPTS

Demand
Quantity demanded
Nonprice determinants of demand

RELATED CONTENT AREAS

Mathematics (graphs)
Language arts
Current events

OBJECTIVES

◆ Define quantity demanded.

◆ Define demand.

◆ Give examples of changes in demand due to changes in consumer tastes and preferences, consumer income, number of consumers, and prices of related goods and services.

◆ Identify an increase or decrease on a graph.

◆ Predict an increase or decrease in demand when given pertinent information.

◆ Give examples of situations in which demand shifts and explain what causes these shifts.

LESSON DESCRIPTION

This lesson gives students the opportunity to study the nonprice determinants of demand and their effect on the demand for products.

TIME REQUIRED

◆ Two class periods

MATERIALS

Visual 1, *Demand Schedule for Bubble Soda*
□ Activity 1, *Bubble Soda Graph* and Activity 2, *Demand Shifters*, for each student.

PROCEDURE

1. Display transparency of Visual 1, and review the following:
   - What does quantity demanded mean? (The amount of a good or service people are willing and able to buy at a particular price, other things being equal.)
   - What is the quantity demanded at a price of $1.00 (5) $ .25 (20)
   - As price goes down, what happens to the quantity demanded? (increases)
   - As price goes up, what happens to the quantity demanded? (decreases)

2. Remind students that the relationship between price and quantity demanded is inverse and is called the Law of Demand. Demand is the relationship between various prices and the quantities consumers are willing and able to buy during some time period, holding all other things constant. Demand is the entire schedule, not a single price and quantity demanded from the schedule.

3. Distribute a copy of Activity 1 to each student. Explain that the activity includes the demand schedule for Bubble Soda and a blank graph.

4. Review:
   - What is another way to illustrate the demand for a product? (graphically)

• How do you graph demand? (By placing price on the vertical axis and quantity on the horizontal axis and plotting the pairs in the schedule.)

5. Instruct students to graph the demand schedule for Bubble Soda, connect the points, and label the curve D. Discuss:

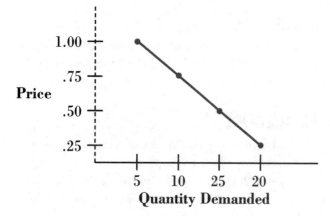

• What does the demand curve look like? (It is downward sloping.)

• Why is the curve downward sloping? (Because as the price goes down the quantity demanded goes up and as price goes up the quantity demanded goes down.)

Option: Using masking tape, construct the price and quantity axis on the gym floor. Mark the scales with pieces of masking tape. Write "price" on one sheet of paper and "quantity" on another. Tape these to the floor to label each axis. Instruct students to place a piece of masking tape at each ordered-pair point. Place a length of yarn along the points. This is the demand curve for Bubble Soda. When you reach procedure step 10, select four students and instruct one of them to stand on each of the four points with their backs toward the horizontal (quantity) axis. Instruct four other students to mark the new points indicated in the table for procedure step 10. Ask students standing to take a step to their right. Ask students to lay down a piece of yarn along the points and step away from the graph. Continue with procedure step 11. This same activity could be used to demonstrate a decrease in demand (students taking a step to the left.)

6. Remind the class they created a demand schedule for a beverage in Lesson 4, *How Many Will You Buy?* Discuss:

• When we determined the demand for this product, what did we change or vary? (The price of the product.)

• Did the price of the other beverages available change during the time of the survey? (No)

• Did the number of consumers in the classroom-beverage market change? (No, the same number of student consumers remained in the classroom.)

• Did student-consumer incomes change while the survey was conducted? (No)

• Were there any changes (other than changes in price for the beverage) that would change consumer tastes for the product? (No)

7. Distribute a copy of Activity 2 to each student and read together.

8. Explain that this activity describes the factors that are held constant or do not vary when a demand schedule is established. Changes in these nonprice determinants cause the demand for a product to shift so we can call them **demand shifters**. A shift in demand means that the quantity demanded at each and every price will change.

9. As a class, apply the information about demand shifters to the Bubble Soda examples listed here.

• If Bubble Soda was endorsed by a famous celebrity, and its popularity increased, what do you think would happen to the quantity demanded at $1.00? $ .75? $ .50? $ .25? (The quantity demanded at each and every price would increase. In other words, demand would increase.) Why? (Advertising resulted in a change in consumer taste and preference.)

• If students received an increase in their allowances, what do you think would happen to the quantity demanded of Bubble Soda at $1.00? $.75? $.50? $.25? (The quantity demanded at each and every price would increase. In other words, demand would increase.) Why? (An increase in allowance results in a change in consumer income.)

- If Bubble Soda was introduced in another country and became popular, what do you think would happen to the quantity demanded for Bubble Soda at $1.00? $.75? $.50? $.25? (The quantity demanded at each and every price would increase. In other words, demand would increase.) Why? (Because there are more consumers in the market for Bubble Soda.)

- If the price of Bola Cola (a substitute for Bubble Soda) increases, what will happen in the market for Bubble Soda? Why? (Demand for Bubble Soda will increase because the price of a substitute good increased.)

10. Write the following table on the board. Explain that more Bubble Soda is being sold at each and every price due to a change in one or more of the demand shifters. Instruct students to graph this new schedule on the Bubble Soda graph and label the new curve D^1.

Price	Quantity Demanded (in thousands)
$ 1.00	10
.75	15
.50	20
.25	25

11. Discuss:
    - If the amount being sold increases at each and every price, what has happened? (Demand increased.)
    - Describe the location of the new demand curve relative to the original

curve. (It has shifted to the right of the original curve.)

12. Explain that when demand changes (increases or decreases) the demand curve shifts. With an increase in demand, the curve shifts to the right.

13. Ask students what they think will happen to the position of the demand curve relative to the original curve, if the demand for Bubble Soda decreases? (It will shift to the left of the original curve.)

14. Refer students to Activity 2, and ask them what things might occur that would cause a decrease in demand. (Answers could include examples of a negative change in consumer tastes, decrease in the number of consumers, and decrease in consumers' incomes.)

15. As a class, apply the information about demand shifters to the Bubble Soda examples given below.
    - If cans of Bubble Soda were contaminated with a harmful chemical and its popularity decreased, what do you think would happen to the quantity demanded of Bubble Soda at $1.00? $.75? $.50? $.25? (The quantity demanded at each and every price would decrease. In other words, demand would decrease.) Why? (Report of contamination changes consumer tastes and preferences.)
    - If each student's allowance is reduced, what do you think would happen to the quantity demanded of Bubble Soda at $1.00? $.75? $.50? $.25? (The quantity demanded at each and every price would decrease. In other words, demand would decrease.) Why? (A decrease in allowance results in a change in consumer income.)

16. Divide the class into groups. Assign each group a demand shifter from the list. Instruct the group to write two examples

of situations that would change demand involving the demand shifter assigned.

17. Ask a spokesperson from each group to read the group's examples. After the situation has been read, ask the other students in the class to give a "thumbs up" if the situation would cause an increase in demand and a "thumbs down" if it would cause a decrease in demand.

CLOSURE

1. Ask students to define demand.

2. Read the following scenarios (or situations) and ask students to give a "thumbs up" if demand would increase and a "thumbs down" if demand would decrease. Ask students to explain why demand would increase or decrease.

   • Schools across the country stop using textbooks. What will happen in the market for textbooks? Why? (Demand will decrease because there will be fewer consumers in the market.)

   • Doctors have excellent results using vitamin E to cure acne. What will happen in the market for vitamin E? Why? (Demand will increase because there is a change in consumer tastes and preferences.)

   • A law is passed guaranteeing students ages 10 and older a minimum allowance of $10.00 per week. What will happen in the market for compact discs? Why? (Demand will increase because consumer income increases.)

   • The price of Bola Cola (a substitute for Bubble Soda) decreases. What will happen in the market for Bubble Soda? Why? (Demand for Bubble Soda will decrease because the price of a substitute good decreases.)

EVALUATION

1. As a class, discuss the goods and services students buy. Divide the class into groups of two or three. Assign each group one of the products listed. Instruct the group to write a situation that exemplifies a change

in demand using three of the demand shifters. Instruct them to write the answers on a separate sheet. Collect the examples and answers and check them for accuracy. Later, distribute the examples to different groups. Instruct students to explain whether the examples would cause an increase or a decrease in the demand for the product and why. Collect answers and return them to the authoring group to be corrected.

2. Ask students to draw graphs illustrating the increase or decrease in demand for each example their group wrote.

EXTENSION

1. Ask students to write headlines illustrating the five demand shifters. Write the best examples with markers on colored paper to create a newspaper front-page bulletin board. Write short news stories to fit under each headline.

2. The current group of adolescents represent the "Baby Bounce." As attention moves away from the Baby Boomers, many manufacturers are recognizing the buying power of teens. Ask students to select one of the goods or services discussed in the lesson. Instruct them to write about the product, relating it to the demand shifters.

3. Instruct students to look through newspapers and magazines for articles and ads related to the demand shifters for a product. (Famous athlete advertising a product: change in tastes and preference; article about need for more skilled nursing care: change in the number of consumers in the market; article about cancer causing agent: change in consumer tastes and preferences; article about increase in taxes: change in consumer incomes.)

4. Have students design a mall of the future that caters to the tastes and preferences of teens. Their drawing or floor plan should be labeled to reflect any trends they anticipate.

VISUAL 1
DEMAND SCHEDULE FOR BUBBLE SODA

Price	Quantity Demanded (in thousands)
$ 1.00	5
.75	10
.50	15
.25	20

Name _____
ACTIVITY 1
BUBBLE SODA GRAPH

Price	Quantity Demanded (in thousands)
$ 1.00	5
.75	10
.50	15
.25	20

DEMAND CURVE FOR BUBBLE SODA

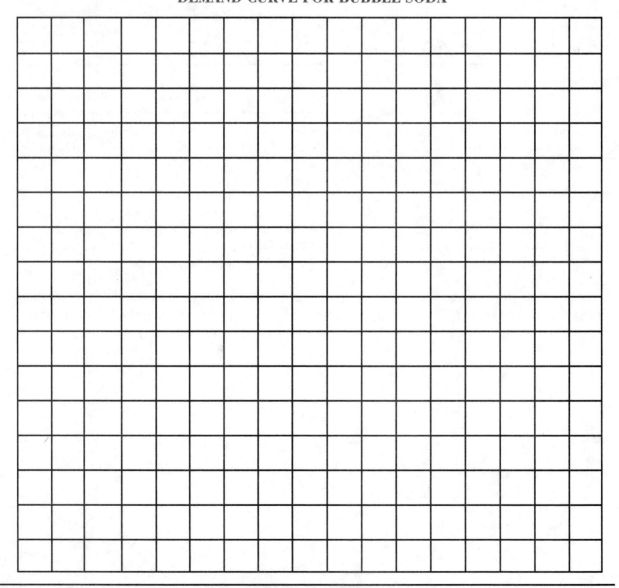

ACTIVITY 2
DEMAND SHIFTERS

Nonprice determinants of demand influence the demand for a product. A change in any of these factors will change the amount consumers are willing and able to buy at each and every price. This constitutes a change in demand.

1. **Change in the number of consumers in the market for a product**

   If the number of consumers in the market for a product increases, the demand for the product will increase. If the number of consumers in the market for a product decreases, the demand for the product will decrease. If a new high school is built in the same block as a fast-food restaurant, the demand for the fast-food restaurant's products will increase. If an automobile manufacturing plant near the fast food restaurant closes, the demand for the restaurant's products will decrease.

2. **Change in consumer tastes and preferences for a product**

   If consumer tastes and preferences for a product change, the demand for the product will change. If fashion magazines are showing short skirts, the demand for short skirts will increase. If fashion magazines show few pictures of short skirts, the demand for these skirts will decrease.

3. **Change in consumer income**

   If consumer income increases (decreases), demand for most goods and services will increase (decrease). For example, if workers at a manufacturing facility sign a new contract that provides a 5% raise, these workers will have more income and their demand for goods and services will increase. If social security taxes increase for employees, consumers will have less take-home pay, and as a result, their demand for goods and services will decrease.

4. **Change in the price of related goods**

   A change in the price of one good can change the demand for another good. One type of related goods are complements—goods that are purchased together. A decrease in the price of strawberries will cause an increase in the demand for whipped cream. An increase in the price of hamburger will cause a decrease in the demand for hamburger buns.

Another type of related goods are substitutes—goods that are bought in place of one another. If the price of movie tickets increases, the demand for video rentals may increase. If the price of Lisa's hamburgers decreases, the demand for Tim's hamburgers may decrease.

INFLATION

INTRODUCTION

Although many factors may contribute to inflation in the short run, inflation can be sustained in an economy over an extended period only by allowing the supply of money to increase faster than the growth of output. Inflation can be simulated in the classroom with the following auction activity.

ECONOMIC CONCEPTS

Inflation

RELATED CONTENT AREAS

Language arts

OBJECTIVES

- ◆ Define inflation as an increase in the average price level.
- ◆ Explain an increase in the money supply may cause inflation.
- ◆ Predict the impact of inflation on purchasing power.

LESSON DESCRIPTION

In this lesson, students participate in two auction rounds to learn about inflation.

TIME REQUIRED

- ◆ One class period

MATERIALS

Two sets of three identical items (for example, a candy bar, pencil, bag of candy)
One small bag of lima beans
One small bag of split peas or lentils
Visual 1, *Auction Report*

PROCEDURE

1. Give each student 4-12 lima beans. Do not give each student the same amount.

2. Announce you will be conducting an auction. Show the first set of three items.

3. Explain students will be able to purchase the items using the lima beans they have been given. Each lima bean has a value of $ .25. Instruct students to calculate how much money they have.

4. Auction each of the three items to the highest bidder. Display Visual 1 and record items and auction prices.

5. "Expand" the money supply in the classroom by giving each student a small handful of the second type of dried seed.

6. Announce you will again conduct an auction. Show the second set of three items.

7. Explain that students will be able to purchase the items using the lima beans and the second type of dried seed. Each bean/seed has a value of $ .25. Instruct students to calculate how much money they have.

8. Auction each of the three items to the highest bidder. Again, record each item and auction price on the board.

9. Discuss:
   - Why were the beans valuable? (Because they could be used to purchase goods in class.)
   - In each auction, what were students attempting to do? (Spend their money on the goods available.)
   - In the second auction, what happened to the price of each item? (Went up.)
   - In the second auction, what happened to the amount of money each student had to spend? (Increased.)
   - What happened to the number of products available in each auction? (Remained the same.)
   - Why do you think students were willing to pay more in the second round? (They had more money to spend and

there were not any more goods or services available.)

10. Explain that in this example, students experienced inflation. Inflation means that, on average, prices of goods and services increase. Prices of some goods and services may not rise, or may even fall, but the average price level is rising.

CLOSURE

1. Explain that in the second auction, each student had more money but there were not anymore goods and/or services available to buy. When there is more money circulating in the economy (the classroom in this case) but the same number of goods and services, inflation occurs. Inflation affects different people in different ways. Sometimes people are worse off; sometimes they are better off.

2. Ask students if their allowance is $5.00 a week and the economy experiences inflation, will they be able to buy more or fewer goods and services? (Fewer.) Why? (You only have $5.00. If the prices of the products you buy goes up, you won't be able to buy as much.) When inflation occurs, the purchasing power of people's money is reduced. They are able to purchase fewer goods and services with the same amount of money.

EVALUATION

1. Instruct students to answer the following questions:
   - Why is our money valuable? (Because it can be used to purchase goods and services.)
   - What is inflation? (An increase in the average price level.)
   - How does inflation affect the purchas-

ing the power of money? (Reduces the purchasing power of money.)

2. Ask students to answer the following questions in their *Economics Role Journals* regarding the role of knowledgeable consumer.
   - Is this one of your roles now? If so, how?
   - How will you fill this role in the future?
   - How will being a knowledgeable consumer benefit you?
   - How is your role as decision maker related to being a knowledgeable consumer?

EXTENSION

1. Read *All the Money in the World*, by Bill Brittain and use the corresponding lesson in *Economics in Children's Literature* (SPEC Publishers, Inc., St. Louis, MO, 1993).

2. Instruct students to ask household members for prices of items when they were children (such as a gallon of gasoline, a pound of hamburger, a can of soda pop, a candy bar, an ice cream cone, a movie ticket) and family incomes at the time. Discuss price and income changes.

3. Have students look in newspapers or magazines such as *USA Today, Business Week,* and *Money Magazine* for the Consumer Price Index (CPI) report for several quarters. Discuss the reports. Ask students to do some research to find out how the CPI is calculated.

4. Show the third filmstrip from *Once Upon a Dime*, Federal Reserve Bank of New York.

VISUAL 1
AUCTION REPORT

Auction Item	Auction #1 Price	Auction #2 Price
1._____ _____ _____	$	$
2._____ _____ _____	$	$
3._____ _____ _____	$	$

INTRODUCTION TO PRODUCTIVE WORKER

The three lessons in this unit relate to the role of individuals as workers. Workers' roles include all those related to the production of goods and services in our economy. "Workers" include all those who make the production process possible, including managers and entrepreneurs. To understand fully that investment in their own human capital makes them more productive throughout their working lives, students must also understand related concepts such as productivity, supply, and the role of profits.

The first lesson reviews the concept of productive resources—those inputs needed to produce goods and services—and introduces two additional concepts: productivity and investment in capital goods. Students explore the decisions that must be made by firms to remain competitive in the market. Through the study of a firm producing T-shirts, students discover that there may be some immediate costs (layoff of workers) to increasing productivity through capital investment. However, the future benefits (remaining competitive and future growth) are critical not only to the firm but to the economy as a whole. And, consumers benefit when firms are able to keep prices low through increased productivity.

The second lesson involves students in the management of a hypothetical school snack bar to help them understand concepts related to supply. They examine the relationship between price and the quantity supplied as well as factors that change supply. The lesson introduces them to nonprice determinants of supply—changes in input costs, changes in the price of other goods or services the firm might produce, and changes in the number of producers.

The third lesson in this unit deals with profit, the driving force behind a market economy. Profits motivate entrepreneurs and business firms to incur the risks involved in producing goods and services. Students learn how to calculate profit for a bakery and examine the role of profits in encouraging an individual to invest in a business.

THE T-RRIFIC T'S COMPANY: PRODUCTION DECISIONS

INTRODUCTION

Productivity refers to the amount of output per unit of input over a period of time. An increase in productivity may mean producing the same amount with fewer inputs, producing more output with the same inputs, or a combination of these. Companies must look for ways to maintain and increase the level of productivity in order to remain competitive while maintaining profits. One way to accomplish this is through investing in capital goods—machines and tools used in the production process. Technological improvements in capital goods are a leading cause of increases in productivity. However, although capital investment can increase productivity, there are opportunity costs and economic risks involved. This lesson examines the production decisions of a firm and the impact of such decisions on workers, stockholders, and the community.

ECONOMIC CONCEPTS

Productive resources
Natural resources
Human resources
Capital resources
Productivity
Investment in capital goods

RELATED CONTENT

Mathematics
Language arts
Critical thinking

OBJECTIVES

◆ Identify and categorize the productive resources used in making T-shirts.

◆ Define productivity.

◆ Identify investment in capital goods as a way to increase productivity.

◆ Analyze the costs and benefits of increasing productivity through capital investment.

LESSON DESCRIPTION

Students help the managers of a T-shirt company make business decisions about the production process. They analyze the costs and benefits of investing in new capital equipment in order to increase productivity.

TIME REQUIRED

◆ Three or four class periods

MATERIALS

★ Activities 1, *Business Decisions in the T-Shirt Company*, 2, *Take a Stand!*, and 3, *In the Short Run, In the Long Run*

PROCEDURE

1. The day prior to beginning the lesson, ask students to wear their favorite T-shirt to class the next day. (If dress codes preclude wearing T-shirts, have students bring their favorite shirt or bring several T-shirts yourself.)

2. Ask students to identify all the inputs or things used to produce a T-shirt. Have them examine labels to determine material content. (Inputs likely to be named: cotton, polyester, and other fabrics; paint or ink; workers; sewing machines; printing machines; other machinery; factory/building.)

3. Explain that the things used to produce T-shirts are factors of production. Some of these are **natural resources**—things found in or on the earth; some are **human resources**—people performing mental or physical work; and some are **capital resources**—things produced by people and used over and over again to produce other goods.

4. Often there are inputs used in production that were produced by people and are used up in the production of something else. These are called **intermediate goods.**

5. Draw four columns on the board with the headings *Natural Resources, Human Resources, Capital Resources,* and *Intermediate Goods.* Have students list the inputs they identified under the correct heading. (Natural: water, cotton, oil; human: designers, printers, etc.; capital: sewing machine, building, etc.; intermediate goods: cloth, thread.)

   Note: Although cotton and polyester cloth are made from natural resources (cotton and oil, respectively), the cloth itself is not a natural resource. It is likely that water is used in the mixing of dyes or inks used in printing designs on the shirts.

6. Discuss: What makes the T-shirts they are wearing their favorite? Note responses. It is likely that the design/graphics on shirts will be one factor.

7. Introduce the class to the T-Rrific T's Company. Distribute a copy of Activity 1 to each student. Read Part 1 and discuss:
   - What has made the T-Rrific T's so popular? (No two designs the same, logo hidden in the design.)
   - What dilemma is the company facing? (Has an order larger than it can handle with current number of workers and machinery.)
   - What options might the firm have to resolve this problem? (Students should identify at least three options: turn down the order, hire enough workers to handle the order, purchase or lease computer-design and printing equipment to increase productivity.)

8. Using the information given, instruct students to calculate the number of workers the company would have to hire to fill the order. Then have students read Part 2 of Activity 3 and fill in the missing numbers in Tom Chen's chart of production costs. After students have completed this work, discuss:
   - Based on the cost of inputs per T-shirt, which option would you recommend to Tarica Ramirez? (Adding new machinery is the most cost-effective method.)
   - Are there other factors (besides input costs) the company could consider in making a decision? List answers on the chalkboard.
   - Among factors they may wish to consider are:
   ✓Will the computer-generated designs sell as well as the hand-painted ones?
   ✓Can you retrain current workers to be computer operators or will you need new workers with special training?
   ✓Will you be able to find enough workers immediately to hire the labor needed if you don't purchase machines?
   ✓What impact will this have on the company's future? Consider long-term impacts on company growth and employment.
   ✓How will stockholders feel about the decision? Stockholders have invested their money in the firm. They hope the firm will make enough profit to pay them a good return—at least as good as other options—on their stock investment. If not, stockholders might decide to sell their stock. In addition, if the company is not remaining competitive and making profits, stock values will decline.
   - Will any other groups be affected by the company's decision? (Workers who might be laid off, members of the community, consumers.)
   - What impact will the decision have on the community? Remember that wages

help the community's economy as workers make purchases at other businesses.

9. Divide the class into four groups of equal size. One group is to represent management, one group stockholders, one group factory workers, and one group community leaders. Discuss briefly the concerns each group might have in dealing with the production issue.

   * Management: keep stockholders happy; keep workers happy
   * Workers: keep jobs; improve wages
   * Stockholders: increase profits to gain dividends or increase stock value
   * Community: maintain or increase jobs in the community

10. Instruct groups, using the information in Activity 1 and the questions raised in #8 above, to list the costs and benefits of each of the three production options. Explain that groups should keep in mind the impact of each option on the people they represent. They should consider both immediate and future costs and benefits.

11. When groups have finished their deliberations, have them share their findings. Discuss:

    * Are there differences of opinion about the best action to take? Why?
    * Are the differences caused (at least partially) by the differing concerns of each role group?
    * What are some of the short-term costs?
    * Are short-term costs offset by long-term benefits? Explain.

CLOSURE

1. Distribute copies of Activity 2 to each student. Using the guidelines and the information from their group discussions, have each group prepare a three-minute presentation to the president of the firm making a recommendation for action. The presentation should include arguments supporting the recommendations based on an explanation of the future and immediate costs and benefits of the proposed action.

EVALUATION

1. Distribute copies of Activity 3 to each student and read directions. You may wish to have the class do the first web together.

2. Have each student write a business memo to the president of T-Rrific T's making a recommendation and explaining his or her decision. The explanation should include an analysis of the immediate and future costs and benefits.

3. Have students interview local business owners or managers about things they have done to increase the productivity of their firms. Be sure the students ask about the impact the firm's actions have had on various people involved—management, workers.

EXTENSION

1. Have students produce T-shirt designs on paper by hand (both original and copies). Then have them use mechanical means to duplicate the process by copying designs or using computer software. Discuss the pros and cons of each process, in terms of productivity and other factors. If facilities are available, students may wish to design real T-shirts.

2. Discuss how the T-Rrific T's decision might be changed if these events are encountered:

   * Cost of labor increases due to new benefits negotiated by the workers
   * Cost of using new equipment increases due to new environmental regulations

3. Instruct students to read a biography or a biographical sketch of an inventor/intrepreneur and write a brief paper explain-

ing the impact of the inventor/entrepreneur work on an industry. The paper should include changes in technology, resulting changes in produc-tivity, and impacts on various workers and consumers. Possible sources:

Women Inventors and Their Discoveries, Ethlie Ann Ware and Greg Ptacek (Oliver Press, 1993).

American Profiles: Twentieth Century Inventions, Nathan Aaseng (New York: Facts on File, 1991).

The Story Behind Great Inventions, Elizabeth Rider Montgomery (New York: Dodd, Mead, 1953).

Invention and Technology: Great Lives, Milton Lomask (New York: Charles Scribner's Sons, 1991).

Invention Book, Steven Caney, (New York: Workman Publishing, 1985).

Black Pioneers of Science and Invention, Louis Haver (San Diego: Harcourt Brace Jovanovich, 1992).

Name _____
ACTIVITY 1
BUSINESS DECISIONS IN THE T-SHIRT COMPANY

Part 1:

Tarica Ramirez, president and founder of the T-Rrific T's Company, is facing a decision that will affect the future of the company. T-Rrific T's started two years ago in Ramirez's basement, where she designed and hand painted colorful T-shirts. Two things make the T-Rrific T's popular: no two designs are exactly alike and each design has the company logo—T$_R$T—hidden in the design.

The shirts sold quickly in a local market, and she hired some friends to help produce more shirts to keep up with the demand. Demand kept growing and over the past year she has hired a few more workers and moved into an old warehouse. Three local business people bought stock in the company to provide the funds needed to expand. The firm currently has one designer, six painters to reproduce the designs (with slight variations on each shirt), and two packers who ship the shirts to area stores. These workers can produce 400 shirts a week, working 40 hours a week. The shirts currently sell for $20 each.

T-Rrific T's has just received an order for 20,000 shirts on the condition they be completed in 16 weeks. If they can fill this order, they have a commitment from the customer for additional orders of 20,000 every four months.

Ramirez knows the company cannot handle this order with the current number of workers. She calls for a meeting with the manager, Tom Chen, to discuss the options they have.

Part 2:

Chen is delighted to have a chance to share information he has been gathering on new computer graphics and printing machinery. With two computers and four printing machines, they can produce 2000 shirts a week. However, he also knows this means laying off part of their work force, since they would need only two computer operators and four packers with the machinery.

Chen knows Ramirez will want to consider all possibilities, so he gathers information on other options. Here is the information Chen has so far. Help Chen complete this chart to present to his boss.

OPTIONS:

#1: Keep current employment; turn down the order.

#2: Add sufficient painters and designers to fill the order; hire 3 additional designers, 19 additional painters, and 2 additional packers; this work force will be able to produce 1250 shirts/week.

#3: Lease machinery that will reproduce the current process and increase productivity; reduce employment by one half of current force; this combination will be able to produce 2000 shirts/week. The cost to run the machines will be $185 per hour (cost of leasing, maintenance, and utilities).

WORKERS NEEDED:

	# Designers	# Painters	# Packers
Current/Option 1	1	6	2
Option 2/Add Workers	4	25	4
Option 3/Lease Machines	2 (Computer design)	0	4

WAGES (with payroll taxes and benefits):

Designers	$15/hr.
Computer Designers (Option 3)	$20/hr.
Painters	$12/hr.
Packers	$10/hr.

	Total labor cost per hour (wages of all workers for one hour)	# Shirts per hour
Current/Option 1	$107.00	10.00 shirts
Option 2		31.25 shirts
Option 3	$ 80.00	30.00 shirts

PRODUCTION COSTS:
(Calculate the labor costs per shirt; divide Col. 1 above by Col. 2)

	Labor: $/hr (Total)	Labor/shirt (Cost of 1 hr.) (#shirts/hr)	Materials/shirt	Other cost/shirt (Machines/Utilities)
Option 1	$107	$	$4.00	$3.00
Option 2	$400	$	$4.00	$3.00
Option 3	$ 80	$	$4.00	$8.70

TOTAL COST OF PRODUCTION PER SHIRT:
(Add cost per hour of labor, materials, and other—machines, utilities, etc.)

Option 1: _____

Option 2: _____

Option 3: _____

Discussion Questions:

1. Based on the production costs per shirt, which option would you recommend?

2. How would that decision affect current workers? Would any new people be hired?

3. What might happen to the company in the long run if they choose Option 1 (turning down the large order)?

4. Besides laying off some workers, are there other negative factors related to choosing Option 3? Do the positive factors outweigh any negatives? Why or why not? (Be sure to think about long-run impacts as well as immediate impacts.)

5. Which decision do you think would be supported by the following groups?
     Management
     Stockholders
     Current workers
     Community leaders
     Unemployed people in the community
     Consumers

Name _____
ACTIVITY 2
TAKE A STAND?

Your group, representing the _____, has studied all the data presented by the manager of T-Rrific T's (see Activity 1). Using this data, you must decide on the option you would recommend to the company. Be sure to consider the future impact of the recommendation as well as immediate effects.

Your group has been asked to make a presentation to the president of the T-Rrific T's Company. The presentation should be three minutes long and should make a good argument for the option your group thinks the company should adopt. Include information about the immediate impact of the action as well as the long-term impact. Be sure you note both positive and negative effects and an explanation of why you recommend this option.

Name _____
ACTIVITY 3
IN THE SHORT RUN, IN THE LONG RUN

Directions:
   In the center circle, place the option you recommended to the T-shirt company. Then, in the other circles, note who is affected and how. Do a web for each of the other options as well.

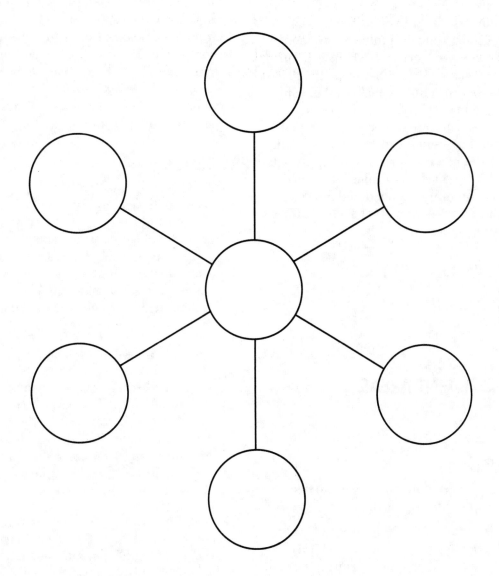

HOW MANY SHOULD WE SELL?

INTRODUCTION

A supply schedule is a table which shows the relationship between the price of a product and the amount of the product producers are willing and able to sell. The entire schedule shows the supply in a given market; the amount at any one price shows the quantity supplied at that price. In the short run, the quantity supplied will increase as price increases. Changes in other factors, such as production costs or the price of other products producers might make, will cause a change in supply. These factors are called nonprice determinants. For example, if labor costs increase significantly, firms will supply less at each and every price, and supply will decrease. This lesson shows students how price changes affect quantity supplied and how changes in input prices and other factors affect the supply of products in a market.

ECONOMIC CONCEPTS

Supply
Quantity supplied
Price
Nonprice determinants of supply

RELATED CONTENT AREAS

Mathematics (graphs)
Language arts

OBJECTIVES

◆ Explain the relationship between price and the quantity supplied.

◆ Identify nonprice determinants of supply.

◆ Predict the impact on supply of changes in nonprice determinants of supply.

LESSON DESCRIPTION

Students learn to predict the impact on supply of nonprice determinants and to differentiate between changes in supply and changes in quantity supplied.

TIME REQUIRED

◆ Three class periods

MATERIALS

☐ Activity 1, *To Market, To Market*, for each student
★ Activity 2, *Company Cards*, cut apart
★ Activity 3, *Situation Cards*, cut apart (five sets)
Visual 1, *Supply Schedule*, and Visual 2, *Supply Graphs*
1 large jar of peanut butter, divided into 10 small paper cups
2 signs: one, *Peanut Butter Fudge Logs* and the other *Cracker Snacks*
Optional: supply of small cheese crackers with peanut butter; peanut butter fudge logs

PROCEDURE

1. Set up a table with 10 small paper cups filled with peanut butter; place five on one half of the table and five on the other half. Place signs on each half of the table, one reading *Cracker Snacks* and the other reading *Peanut Butter Fudge Logs*. If desired, have samples of each snack item on display. (See extension activities for details.)

2. Provide the following scenario:

3. The eighth-grade class at King School has decided to sell snacks during the lunch hour. A survey of students in the school indicates that two kinds of peanut butter snacks would sell well: Peanut Butter Cracker Snacks and Peanut Butter Fudge Logs.

3. Ask for a volunteer to be manager of the school snack bar. Tell the manager that he or she will be making some decisions about the production of snacks for sale in the school. Since the entire class will benefit from any profits, they will help make the decisions. Tell students they need to put on their "producer hats" and think like business owners, not consumers.

4. Have five students go to the table as employees of the Cracker Snack production unit; have five more go as employees of the Peanut Butter Fudge Logs production unit. Remind the students that the peanut butter and the workers are productive resources or inputs that could be used to produce either item.

5. Explain that each employee can produce 10 items with one paper cup of peanut butter. Right now, it costs 30 cents to produce each item, and both products will sell at 40 cents. At this time, the company is producing an equal amount of each product.

6. Discuss:
   * With the inputs divided the way they are now, how many Cracker Snacks can you make? Peanut Butter Fudge Logs? (Answer for each is 50.)
   * If a market survey shows that you should sell each product at 40 cents, how much profit will you make per item? (10 cents revenue per unit of 40 cents minus costs per unit of 30 cents.)
   * If you switched all the resources to make just one of the items, how many could you produce of that item each day? (100) What would you give up? (Producing the other product.)

7. Ask the manager (with class help) what production changes he or she might make if the following events occur. Employees and cups should be moved from one end of the table to the other to represent each decision. Ask another student to record the changes on the board, noting the number of resources being used for Crackers and for Peanut Butter Fudge Logs for each event, A, B, and C. After resources are switched and noted, have the class calculate how much of each product would be produced under each circumstance.
   A. An increase in consumer demand makes it possible to sell Peanut But-ter Fudge Logs for 60 cents each. (Students will probably want to switch at least some resources from Cracker Snacks to Peanut Butter Fudge Logs to increase the quantity supplied of Fudge Logs and gain greater profits.)
   B. The price of crackers goes up, increasing production costs to 40 cents per item for Cracker Snacks. (Students probably will no longer want to make Cracker Snacks, because there is no profit; they are likely to switch all resources to Peanut Butter Fudge Logs where profit is 30 cents.)
   C. A local firm decides to donate the crackers needed for production, reducing production costs on Cracker Snacks to 10 cents each. (Probably students will switch more production to Cracker Snacks; if they sell for 40 cents, profit is 30 cents each.)

(Students may return to seats after this activity has been completed.)

8. Discuss:
   * Why did you shift productive resources in each case? (To increase profit.)
   * What happened when the price of a product increased (first event)? (Decided to produce and sell more of the product.)

9. Display Visual 1 with only one supply schedule showing. Discuss:
   * Look at the supply schedule. Would you be willing to sell either of your products at the lowest price? Why or why not? (No, would lose money because production costs are higher than the price.)
   * Would you be willing to sell either of your products at the next lowest price? Why or why not? (Repeat for each price.)

- Would you be willing to sell more at $1.00 than at 80 cents? At 80 cents than at 60 cents? At 60 cents than at 40 cents? (Answers should be yes to each.)

10. Explain that the **Law of Supply** says that as price increases, the quantity supplied will increase. They have just shown that, since they were willing to sell more at higher prices than at lower prices. Show all of Visual 1:

Supply Schedule for Cracker Snacks

Price	Quantity Supplied
$1.00	100
.80	80
.60	60
.40	40
.20	20

Supply Schedule for Peanut Butter Fudge Logs

Price	Quantity Supplied
$1.00	100
.80	80
.60	60
.40	50
.20	0

11. Explain that the prices and quantities to be sold make up a **supply schedule,** which shows the relationship between price and quantity supplied. The supply schedules on the visual are possible supply schedules in the market for Cracker Snacks and the market for Peanut Butter Fudge Logs. The amount offered at any one price is the **quantity supplied;** the whole schedule shows the **supply** of each item in the market. Discuss: What trend do you see in this schedule? (As price increases, sellers are willing to offer more of the product for sale.)

12. Using Visual 2, graph the results of both supply schedules. Tell the students that each graph shows a **supply curve;** each is a picture of a supply schedule, showing how many snacks would be offered at every price. Remind students that changes in quantity supplied are caused only by changes in price (the quantity supplied of Peanut Butter Fudge Logs increased when the price of Peanut Butter Fudge Logs increased). When price changes, the quantity supplied changes. This price and quantity is represented by a different mark on the same supply curve.

Supply of Cracker Snacks

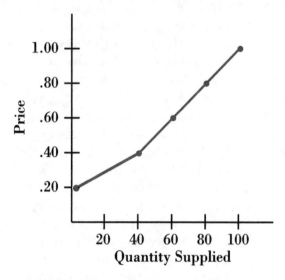

Supply of Peanut Butter Fudge Logs

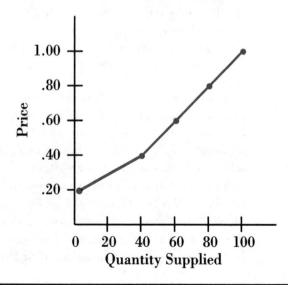

13. Have students locate the point on the supply curve for Peanut Butter Fudge Logs at which they would be producing when the activity began (Q^S=50). Ask the students what production change they made when the price at which they could sell Peanut Butter Fudge Logs went up? (They produced more Peanut Butter Fudge Logs.) Using that price on the supply schedule, mark the change on the supply curve for Fudge Logs (Q^S=60). Explain that when the price of the product changes, quantity supplied (not supply) changes, and the movement is shown on the same supply curve.

14. Discuss:
    • When the cost of production for Cracker Snacks went down (free crackers), did the price change? (No; it was still 40 cents.)
    • How can we show this change on our graph? (Let students make suggestions.) Have a student find the price at which they are selling Cracker Snacks on the price axis.
    • If we know they are now going to offer more than 50 units for sale, where would the quantity supplied have to be marked to show an increase? (It will have to be somewhere to the right of the original supply curve; use the number from their production decision in 7C and mark that point on the supply graph for Cracker Snacks.) Obviously, this point is not on the original supply curve but is part of another supply curve that represents an increase in supply.

15. Explain that if things other than price change, **supply** will shift (sellers will offer more or less at all prices). These other factors are called **nonprice determinants** or **supply shifters.** They include such things as changes in input costs (the free crackers), changes in the price of other goods the firm could produce (the increase in price of Peanut Butter Fudge Logs will cause the supply

of Cracker Snacks to decline), and a change in the number of suppliers in the market.

16. On the graph for Cracker Snacks, draw a line parallel to the original supply curve through the point identified in #12 above. This shows a change (increase) in supply of Cracker Snacks—the producer is willing to sell more of these at each price because, since input costs went down, the profit on each item is more.

17. Ask students how they could show the change that occurred in Cracker Snacks when the price of Peanut Butter Fudge Logs increased. (It causes a decrease in supply of Cracker Snacks, moving the supply curve up and to the left.) Note that this is another nonprice determinant for Cracker Snacks (price of the Cracker Snacks did not change; the change in supply was brought about by a price change in *another* product, Peanut Butter Fudge Logs).

18. Summarize with the following: changes in the price of the product will affect the quantity supplied by producers; changes in supply shifters will affect the total supply in each market.

CLOSURE

1. Read the following statements/questions to the class. Have groups decide whether the event will cause a change in *quantity supplied,* or in *supply* of the product and whether that change will be an increase or a decrease. Students should be able to explain their responses.
    • The price of sugar goes up. What will happen in the market for sugar?
      Answer: Quantity supplied will increase.
      When the price of the product changes, the quantity supplied changes. The law of supply tells us that as price increases, quantity supplied increases.
    • The price of sugar goes up. What will happen in the market for candy?

Answer: Supply will decrease.

Sugar is an input in the production of candy. An increase in the cost of an input raises the costs of production. An increase in the costs of production causes a decrease in supply.

- A new candy company begins production in the market. What will happen in the market for candy?

  Answer: Supply will increase.

  An increase in the number of producers of a product will cause an increase in the supply of that product.

- The price of jelly beans goes up. What will happen in the market for red hots?

  Answer: Supply will decrease.

  An increase in the price of another product a firm can produce will encourage them to begin producing a larger quantity of that product (jelly beans) and to reduce the supply of another product they could produce (red hots).

- The workers in the athletic shoe factory get a wage increase. What will happen in the market for athletic shoes?

  Answer: Supply will decrease.

  An increase in the costs of production (labor) will cause a decrease in supply.

- New machinery reduces the cost of making shoes. What will happen in the market for athletic shoes?

  Answer: Supply will increase.

  A reduction in the costs of production (through increased productivity/technology) will lead to an increase in supply.

EVALUATION

1. Hand out copies of Activity 1 to each student. Have students working in small groups, write five situations and questions, using the format above. Two situations should describe events that affect quantity supplied; three should describe events that affect supply. Each student should write the group's examples on his or her activity sheet.

Then, have each group read situations and questions to the class. Make any necessary changes to assure that the questions go appropriately with the statements. Again, students should make changes suggested on their papers. Collect and redistribute the papers so that students do not have their own. Answer the sample questions together. (*Supply will decrease because the cost of an input has gone up.*) Then have the students provide answers and explanations for the statements on the paper they receive. Discuss results.

2. Divide the class into five "companies" that will be producers and sellers of compact discs. Provide each company with a card (Activity 2) indicating costs of production and the supply schedule for their firm. (Point out that at the time this lesson was written, the market price for a CD was typically $15.)

3. Discuss:
   - What trend do you see in your supply schedule? (As price increases, sellers are willing to offer more of the product for sale—that is, quantity supplied increases with price.)
   - Why didn't any company want to sell its product at $10? (Costs of production for all the firms exceed $10; they would lose money.)
   - Why did some firms sell at $12.00, but not all of them? (The price was still below production costs for some of the firms, but was enough to make a small profit for others.)
   - Why did supply schedules for each firm differ? (Production costs differed.)

4. Hand out Situation Card 1 (from Activity 3) to each group and have them read it.

   Ask:
   - Does this event change the quantity of CDs your firm will provide or does it shift your firm's supply? (shifts supply)

- Will supply increase or decrease because of this event? (decrease)
- Why? (Costs of production will increase; producers will not find it worthwhile to supply as many compact discs at the current price.)

5. Repeat the process with Situation Cards 2, 3, and 4.
   - Card 2: quantity supplied, increases; law of supply: as price increases, quantity supplied increases.
   - Card 3: shifts supply; increase; more producers in the market
   - Card 4: shifts supply; decrease; producers can make greater profit by producing the product with the higher price, as long as production costs for producing CD-Rom discs and compact discs remain about the same

6. Have students draw graphs of their original supply curve for their firm; then show on the graph the changes occurring from each event on the Situation Cards.

EXTENSION

1. If Production Worker: Lesson 7, The T-Rrific T's Company: Production Decisions has been used, have students develop a supply schedule based on T-Trific T's production costs. Graph the supply curve.

   Have students think of situations that would change supply or quantity supplied for the T-Rrific T's company.

2. Have students look for newspaper headlines or stories in news magazines that describe a situation or event that would have an impact on the supply or the quantity supplied in a market. Use these as a basis for discussion.

3. Make the Cracker Snacks or Peanut Butter Fudge Logs.

   Cracker Snacks:

   Using cheese-flavored crackers or wheat crackers, spread 1 tsp. peanut butter on one cracker and top with a second cracker.

   Peanut Butter Fudge Logs:

   Mix together 2 cups crunchy peanut butter, 1 lb. powdered sugar, 1 stick margarine (melted), and 6 cups Rice Krispies. Form mixture into small "logs" about $1^{1}/_{2}$ to 2 inches long. Place on cookie sheet and chill in refrigerator. Melt one 12 oz. bag of chocolate chips in a double boiler; spread on top of each log or dip one side into chocolate. Chill again until chocolate is firm.

ACTIVITY 1
TO MARKET, TO MARKET

Instructions: As a group, write five situations that will affect either quantity supplied or supply. Then write questions about how the change affects the market. Two statements should be situations that affect the quantity supplied; three should be situations that affect supply. Mix the statements up. A sample situation/question is given. Be sure to write all five situations and questions your group develops on your own paper.

Sample Statement/?: The price of leather goes up. What will happen in the market for leather shoes?

Answer: _____

_____

1. Statement /?: _____

_____

Answer: _____

_____

2. Statement /?: _____

_____

Answer: _____

_____

3. Statement /?: _____

_____

Answer: _____

_____

4. Statement /?: _____

_____

Answer: _____

_____

5. Statement /?: _____

_____

Answer: _____

ACTIVITY 2
COMPANY CARDS

Note to the teacher: Student groups may wish to name their company

COMPANY A: _____

Your company is able to produce 10,000 compact discs per week; the cost of production per disc is $11.50. The resources you have (capital equipment, labor, natural resources, and intermediate goods) could also be used to produce discs for CD-ROM programs. Your supply schedule is:

Price	Q_s
$ 10.00	0
12.00	2,000
14.00	4,000
16.00	6,000
18.00	8,000
20.00	10,000

COMPANY B: _____

Your company is able to produce 10,000 compact discs per week; the cost of production per disc is $12.65. The resources you have (capital equipment, labor, natural resources, and intermediate goods) could also be used to produce discs for CD-ROM programs. Your supply schedule is:

Price	Q_s
$ 10.00	0
12.00	0
14.00	3,000
16.00	5,000
18.00	8,000
20.00	10,000

COMPANY C: _____

Your company is able to produce 10,000 compact discs per week; the cost of production per disc is $11.00. The resources you have (capital equipment, labor, natural resources, and intermediate goods) could also be used to produce discs for CD-ROM programs. Your supply schedule is:

Price	Q_s
$ 10.00	0
12.00	2,000
14.00	3,000
16.00	4,000
18.00	6,000
20.00	8,000

ACTIVITY 2 (continued)

COMPANY D: _____

Your company is able to produce 10,000 compact discs per week; the cost of production per disc is $10.20. The resources you have (capital equipment, labor, natural resources, and intermediate goods) could also be used to produce discs for CD-ROM programs. Your supply schedule is:

Price	Q_s
$ 10.00	0
12.00	3,000
14.00	5,000
16.00	7,000
18.00	9,000
20.00	10,000

COMPANY E: _____

Your company is able to produce 10,000 compact discs per week; the cost of production per disc is $13.50. The resources you have (capital equipment, labor, natural resources, and intermediate goods) could also be used to produce discs for CD-ROM programs. Your supply schedule is:

Price	Q_s
$ 10.00	0
12.00	0
14.00	2,000
16.00	4,000
18.00	7,000
20.00	10,000

ACTIVITY 3
SITUATION CARDS

SITUATION 1:
The workers in your factory have negotiated a new contract that requires the company to pay the cost of health care insurance.

SITUATION 2:
The price of compact discs increases due to increased demand.

SITUATION 3:
Several companies that produce records are starting to produce compact discs.

SITUATION 4:
The price of CD-ROM discs has gone up considerably.

VISUAL 1

Supply Schedule for Cracker Snacks

Price	Quantity Supplied
$1.00	100
.80	80
.60	60
.40	40
.20	20

Supply Schedule for Peanut Butter Fudge Logs

Price	Quantity Supplied
$1.00	100
.80	80
.60	60
.40	50
.20	0

VISUAL 2
SUPPLY GRAPHS

CRACKER SNACKS

PRICE

$1.00

.80

.60

.40

.20

0 10 20 30 40 50 60 70 80 90 100 Qs

FUDGE LOGS

PRICE

$1.00

.80

.60

.40

.20

0 10 20 30 40 50 60 70 80 90 100 Qs

THE PROFIT PUZZLE

INTRODUCTION

The hope of earning profit motivates entrepreneurs and business firms to incur the risks involved in producing goods and services for the market. Profit is the difference between revenues and the costs entailed in producing or selling a good or service; it is a return for risk taking. Profit-seeking firms are the basic production units in a market economy. Businesses make decisions about production based partially on the hope of maximizing profits. The amount of profit a firm makes depends on price, quantity demanded, and the costs of production.

ECONOMIC CONCEPTS

Accounting profit
Economic profit
Costs of production

RELATED CONTENT AREAS

Mathematics
Language arts

OBJECTIVES

◆ Define costs of production, sales revenue, and accounting profit.

◆ Calculate the sales revenue and profit for a good.

◆ Determine from among choices the most profitable output level for a given product.

◆ Explain the function of profits in a market economy.

◆ Predict the impact of changes in sales price and input costs on revenue and profits.

LESSON DESCRIPTION

Students help Pierre determine which items to continue to sell in his bakery, based on identifying the most profitable items. The concepts are reinforced as students make similar decisions for opening a school snack bar.

TIME REQUIRED

◆ 2 class periods

MATERIALS

★ Activities 1, *Prices and Profits*; 2, *Pierre's Product Picks*; and 3, *The Student Snack Shack* for each student

Visuals 1, *Prices and Profits: Answers*, 2, *Pierre's Product Picks*; Answers, and 3, *The Student Snack Shack*; Answers
Calculators

PROCEDURE

1. Discuss how students might use $30,000. (Options include: place in a savings account, buying stocks and bonds, buying precious metals, and so on.) People have many options regarding the use of their money. Investing in a business is one of the options. But, people will do this only if they think the business (their own or someone else's) will make a profit. In other words, they expect a return on their investment. Explain that profit is the motivating factor for a business to take the risks of producing goods or services.

2. Define accounting profit: Profit = Sales Revenue − Costs of Production. Define sales revenue and costs of production: Sales revenue = Price × Quantity Demanded; Costs of production include costs of all inputs (productive resources) used in the production process (wages and benefits, raw materials, capital equipment, utilities, and so on).

3. Ask students how much profit they think most businesses make as a percentage of total sales: 5%? 15%? 20%? 40%? (Answers will vary.) (Note that the average for a U.S. business is around 4–5%. Figures vary from one type of business to another. For example, grocery store profit on sales is only about 1%; figures for other types of retail firms include clothing, 4.1%; stereo equipment, 4.5%; fast food, 5.8%.)

---

4. Distribute a copy of Activity 1 to each student and read the background scenario.

   Note: Pierre invested $30,000 of his own money to start his business. He used the money to buy a building and equipment. He manages the business and works long hours to make it successful but does not pay himself a salary. The profits the business earns are his to use as he sees fit.

5. Have students work independently to complete the chart. Display transparency of Visual 1 and discuss the results.

   - If his current price is $1.50, will Pierre's sales revenues increase by raising the price? (No; it decreases at both $1.75 and at $2.00.)

   - What caused his sales revenue to decrease? (Consumers were very responsive to the change in price. The quantity demanded decreased by a large number.)

   - At what price does Pierre make the most profit on his Pecan Puffs? (The current price, $1.50.)

   - What other impact might there be if Pierre raises his price on this item? (If other area bakeries are selling similar items at a lower price, customers may go to those places.)

   - Would you recommend that Pierre raise the price on Pecan Puffs? (Unless other factors change, he should keep the price at $1.50.)

   (See Lesson 4, *How Many Will You Buy?* for more information on the effect of higher prices on quantity demanded.)

6. Tell students: Since raising the current price on this item does not appear to be a good way to increase his profits, Pierre decides he could improve his profit by eliminating items on which profit is low and concentrate on producing and selling those items on which profit is higher. The resources now being used on the low-profit items could be switched to producing more of the high-profit items. Pierre is sure that many of his consumers will switch from the items he drops to other items he continues. Help Pierre find which of his bakery items are most profitable.

7. Hand out Activity 2 to all students. Have them work in groups of 4-5 to complete the information on the chart. If necessary, review how to calculate sales revenue and profit. Note that the sales figures on the chart are for three months of business.

CLOSURE

1. When students have finished their work, display transparency of visual and discuss results.

   - Which six items make the highest profit for Pierre? (Doughnut Delights, Cocoa Cubes, Chocolate Clouds, Cinnamon Curls, Sweet Nothings, and Super Cinnamon Rolls.)

   - Which three items make the least profit? (Buttery Bread Sticks, Apple Tarts, and Paris Pound Cake.)

   - Do you think he should continue to sell the Pecan Puffs and Chez Cherree? (Answers will vary; although they are not as high-profit as some items, they are popular; dropping them may mean losing customers.) Should Pierre continue to sell Buttery Bread Sticks? (Answers will vary; again, it is a lower-profit item, but not nearly as low as Apple Tarts and Paris Pound Cake. Since the Bread Sticks are the only non-sweet item on his list and are very popular, he may decide to keep selling them.)

   - What might happen in each of these cases:

     ✓the price of ingredients for the Super Cinnamon Rolls and Pierre's Pecan Puffs increase. (Profits on those items will decrease.)

     ✓the cost of health insurance benefits for all his employees goes up. (Costs of production will increase and profits will decrease.)

✓the cost of ingredients for Buttery Bread Sticks decreases. (The profit on this item will increase.)

2. How much profit did Pierre make in one year (include all items)? ($25,840) Is this high enough profit to keep Pierre in this business? (Since Pierre is managing the business, puts in long hours of work, and has invested $30,000 of his own money, the profit is a fair return on his investment and a reward for taking the risks of running a business. If he paid himself a salary of $20,000, he is earning $5,840 for investing his money and taking the risks of operating the business. This is economic profit. Economic profit is calculated by including the salary forgone by the business owner. In this case, Pierre could earn $20,000 working elsewhere.)

    *   If he sets aside 20% of his profits for future expenditures at the bakery (to replace equipment, expand, etc.), what is his profit then? ($20,160; if you subtract a "salary" of $20,000, his reward for risk taking and investment is only $160).

    *   Would he be better off working for someone else and keeping his money in the bank? (Answers will vary. He might have been able to put his $30,000 in a savings certificate earning 5% interest and earned a salary of $20,000 working for someone else. His reasons for investing in his own business could include the promise of higher return on his investment than in savings; wanting to be his own boss; possibility of earning more than if he worked for someone else.)

EVALUATION

1. Instruct students to write a memo to Pierre recommending the items he should continue to produce and sell. The memo should include the sales revenue, cost of production, and total profit for the recommended items. The memo should also note the least profitable items. Give reasons for all recommendations. (**Note:** items students recommend may vary, but they should include all of the high-profit items. Answers should be accepted if they can provide good reasons for their choices.)

2. Have students using Activity 3, work in groups or independently to decide which items the students should sell at their new snack bar. Discuss results.

3. Ask students to suggest situations that might change their snack bar sales. They should explain what the changes would be and why. (Examples: Another organization sets up a competing business; cost of popcorn from supplier increases; the nearest store selling snacks to students goes out of business.)

4. Ask students to answer the following questions in their *Economics Role Journal* regarding the role of productive worker.

    *   Is this one of your roles now? If so, how?
    *   How will you fill this role in the future?
    *   How will being a productive worker benefit you?
    *   How is your role as decision maker related to being a productive worker?

EXTENSION

1. Have students calculate the percent of total sales revenue for each of the items in Activity 1. Have students graph the results in a circle graph.

2. Ask the owner of a small business to speak to the class about costs of production, sales revenue, and profit for her or his business.

3. Ask students to write a paragraph answering the question: If you had the choice of putting $30,000 in a savings certificate paying 5% interest, or investing

$30,000 in your own business, which would you choose? (Answers will vary.)

4. Read *The Toothpaste Millionaire* by Jean Merrill (Boston: Houghton Mifflin, 1972). Discuss the cost, price, and profit for Rufus' toothpaste enterprise.

5. Read *LeRoy and the Old Man* and use the corresponding lesson in *Economics and Children's Literautre*, (St. Louis: SPEC Publishers, Inc., 1993).

6. Read *The Store that Mama Built* by Robert Lehrman (New York: Macmillan, 1992). Discuss the revenue, costs of production, and profit for the family.

Name _____
ACTIVITY 1
PRICES AND PROFITS

Background: Pierre's Bakery is doing a good business, but Pierre would like to improve his profits. Some items cost more to produce than others. (They take more labor time to make, have more expensive ingredients, and so on.) He has thought about raising the price on those items, but there are several other bakeries in the area, so he must keep his price close to theirs if he wants to stay competitive. Also, he knows that raising prices will have an effect on how much people will buy. He is not sure whether raising prices on some items will actually increase sales revenue for those items. Pierre decides to use a market survey to see if raising the price of Pierre's Pecan Puffs will increase his sales revenue (and, therefore, his profits). Fill out the chart below to help Pierre find out whether raising prices will increase his sales revenue. (All figures are for three months of business)

PRICES AND PROFITS FOR PIERRE'S PECAN PUFFS

Price	Quantity Demanded	Sales Revenue	Cost of Production	Accounting Profit
$2.00	300	$	$285.00	$
1.75	450		427.50	
1.50	800		760.00	
1.30	1000		950.00	
1.10	1100		1045.00	
1.00	1200		1140.00	

1. What happens to quantity demanded (the amount consumers will buy) when price goes up?

2. Does sales revenue increase as price increases?

3. Does profit increase with each increase in price?

VISUAL 1
Answers
PRICES AND PROFITS

PRICES AND PROFITS FOR PIERRE'S PECAN PUFFS

Price	Quantity Demanded	Sales Revenue	Cost of Production	Accounting Profit
$2.00	300	$ 600.00	$285.00	$315
1.75	450	787.50	427.50	360
1.50	800	1200.00	760.00	440
1.30	1000	1300.00	950.00	350
1.10	1100	1210.00	1045.00	165
1.00	1200	1200.00	1140.00	60

1. What happens to quantity demanded (the amount consumers will buy) when price goes up? (decreases)

2. Does sales revenue increase as price increases? (It does from $1.00 up to $1.30; then it begins to decrease.)

3. Does profit increase with each increase in price? (It does from $1.00 up to $1.50; then profit decreases as prices continue to go up.)

Name _____
ACTIVITY 2
PIERRE'S PRODUCT PICKS

Instructions: Using the information provided, calculate the missing numbers and decide which items make the profit for Pierre. Mark the six most profitable items in the profit column with a (+); mark the three least profitable items with a (-). The figures for Columns 3–6 are for three months at Pierre's Gourmet Bakery.

Item	Price	Quanity Demanded	Sales Revenue	Cost of Production	Profit
Pierre's Pecan Puffs	$1.50	800	$	760	$
Buttery Bread Sticks	.75	1100		605	
Chez Cherree		1.20	1080	675	
Doughnut Delights	.85	2000		1000	
Cocoa Cubes		3000	1500	600	
Apple Tarts	1.00	400		360	
Chocolate Clouds	1.50	200		1000	
Paris Pound Cake	4.00	200		760	
Cinnamon Curls		4000	4000	2000	
Sweet Nothings	.60	5000		2500	
Super Cinnamon Rolls	1.50	1200		1140	

1. Do the highest priced items always provide the highest sales revenue? the highest profit? Why or why not?
2. Do the items that sell the most (quantity demanded) provide the highest revenue? Why or why not?

VISUAL 2
Answers
PIERRE'S PRODUCT PICKS

Item	Price	Quantity Demanded	Sales Revenue	Cost of Production	Profit
Pierre's Pecan Puffs	$1.50	800	$1200	760	$440
Buttery Bread Sticks	.75	1100	825	605	275(-)
Chez Cherree	1.20	900	1080	675	405
Doughnut Delights	.85	2000	1700	1000	700(+)
Cocoa Cubes	.50	3000	1500	600	900(+)
Apple Tarts	1.00	400	400	360	40(-)
Chocolate Clouds	1.50	200	1500	1000	500(+)
Paris Pound Cake	4.00	1000	800	760	40(-)
Cinnamon Curls	1.00	4000	4000	2000	2000(+)
Sweet Nothings	.60	5000	3000	2500	500(+)
Super Cinnamon Rolls	1.50	1200	1800	1140	660(+)

1. Do the highest priced items always provide the highest sales revenue? the highest profit? Why or why not? [*No to both; revenue depends on quantity demanded as well as price; profit depends on costs as well as revenue.*]

2. Do the items that sell the most (quantity demanded) provide the highest revenue? Why or why not? [*No; if price is low, total revenue may not be as high as for some items that sell less in quantity.*]

Name _____
ACTIVITY 3
THE STUDENT SNACK SHACK

Instructions: The seventh graders at Pioneer School have decided to open a snack bar. They will be able to sell items to students before and after school. After doing some market surveys, they have come up with the information below on what items will sell best at prices that will be similar to prices at other stores in the area.

Using the information provided, calculate the missing numbers and decide which items make the most profit for the Snack Shack. Then write a letter to your principal recommending the items that will make the most profit.

(figures are for one month)

Item	Price	Quantity Demanded	Sales Revenue	Cost of Production	Accounting Profit
Doughnuts	$ .60	200	$	$100.00	$
Yogurt	1.00	50		42.50	
Orange juice	1.20	100		100.00	
Fresh fruit	.85	50		25.00	
Nachos	1.75	250		400.00	
Chips (bags)	.75	300		180.00	
Popcorn	.50	500		175.00	
Soda	.50	400		185.00	
Lemonade	.75	100		50.00	
Candy	.40	150		52.50	
Gum	.25	200		30.00	

1. Select 3 items for selling before school and 5 items for selling after school, based on which will provide the greatest profit.
2. Are there any reasons for choosing items to sell that make less profit?

 From *Focus: Middle School Economics*, © National Council on Economic Education, New York, NY

VISUAL 3
Answers
THE STUDENT SNACK SHACK

Item	Price	Quantity Demanded	Sales Revenue	Cost of Production	Accounting Profit
Doughnuts	$ .60	200	$120.00	$100.00	$20.00
Yogurt	1.00	50	50.00	42.50	7.50
Orange Juice	1.20	100	120.00	100.00	20.00
Fresh Fruit	.85	50	42.50	25.00	17.50
Nachos	1.75	250	437.50	400.00	37.50
Chips (bags)	.75	300	225.00	180.00	45.00
Popcorn	.50	500	250.00	175.00	75.00
Soda	.50	400	200.00	185.00	15.00
Lemonade	.75	100	75.00	50.00	25.00
Candy	.40	150	60.00	52.50	7.50
Gum	.25	200	50.00	30.00	20.00

1. Selected 3 items for selling before school and 5 items for selling after school, based on which will provide the greatest profit. (Doughnuts, orange juice, fresh fruit, nachos, chips, popcorn, lemonade, and gum.)
2. Are there any reasons for choosing items to sell that make less profit? (It might be pointed out that soda is a complementary good to popcorn, nachos, and chips. If the stand does not sell soda, popcorn, chip and nacho sales may drop. Therefore, it may be better to sell soda than gum—even though profit is less.)

INTRODUCTION TO RESPONSIBLE CITIZEN

This unit addresses the student's role as responsible citizen. While students do not formally exercise their citizenship in the voting booth until the age of eighteen, preparation for this role begins at a much earlier age. Understanding basic economic content is important to the understanding of public policy. Five lessons in this unit address economic content important for future citizens in making public policy choices.

Lesson 10 introduces students to the categories of federal spending including public goods, transfer payments, and interest on the debt.

Lesson 11 introduces students to the categories of federal taxation and calculation of the percentage of total taxes collected in each category.

In Lesson 12, students look at their consumption of goods and services in a day. They consider household spending for the nation as a portion of gross domestic product.

In Lesson 13, students participate in a "readers' theater" play to learn about gross domestic product.

In Lesson 14, students use a decision tree to analyze a budget problem for a public school and then apply the decision process to a local or national issue that involves voter approval and/or use of public funds.

WHERE DOES THE MONEY GO?

INTRODUCTION

One of the economic functions of government is the production of public goods and services. Public goods are those the government supplies in situations involving nonexclusion and/or shared consumption. Every level of government—federal, state, and local—requires citizens to make payments called taxes that are used for the production of public goods and services and other government activities. This lesson examines the major categories of federal spending and the public goods and services included.

ECONOMIC CONCEPTS

Public goods
Nonexclusion
Shared consumption
Taxes
Categories of spending
Interest

RELATED CONTENT AREAS

Mathematics (percentages, tables, circle graphs, bar graphs)

OBJECTIVES

◆ Define public goods as goods supplied by government in situations involving nonexclusion and/or shared consumption.

◆ Explain that some tax revenues are used to provide public goods and services.

◆ Predict ways in which individuals benefit from public goods.

◆ Recognize that government pays for activities and programs other than public goods with tax revenue.

LESSON DESCRIPTION

Students look at the categories of federal spending, discuss them, and calculate the percentage of spending in each category.

TIME REQUIRED

◆ Two class periods

MATERIALS

○ Activity 1 or dollar bill
  100 pennies for each group of 6 students
  Visual 1, *Where Does the Federal Dollar Go?*, and Visual 2, *A Tell-Tale Table: Answers*
★ Activity 1, *A Tell-Tale Table*, for each student
  Calculator for each group
★ Activity 2, *Federal Spending Circle Graph*, for each student
  Protractor for each student

PROCEDURE

1. As students watch, cut the money from Activity 1 along the marked lines. Give each strip to a student in the class.

2. Ask students to tape their strips to the board and write the percentage the strip represents next to it.

3. Explain that each strip and percentage represents the portion of the federal tax dollar spent on a particular program or activity. Some of these expenditures are for public goods and services.

4. Tell students you have decided to charge each student for light in the classroom. Discuss:

   • How many would be willing to pay for light?

   • How many would not pay?

   • Could those who refuse to pay be excluded from using the light? (No. All of the students are assigned to the class and could not be thrown out for refusing to pay for light.)

   • This is an example of **nonexclusion.** The teacher (producer) cannot withhold light (the good) from the consumers who refuse to pay.

5. Discuss:

   • If students in the front rows receive

illumination from the light, will that prevent others in the class from using the same illumination? (No)

- If students in the back rows receive illumination, will that prevent others in the class from using the same illumination? (No)

- This is an example of **shared consumption**: The consumption of a product or service by one person does not reduce its usefulness to others.

6. Tell students that national defense and interstate highways are examples of public goods the federal government provides. Ask students for other examples.

7. Write "taxes" on the board. Ask students for examples of taxes. (Income, sales, personal property, real estate.) Ask why people pay taxes. (Government requires people to pay taxes.) Define taxes as required payments imposed by government.

8. Explain that governments use some of the tax revenue they collect to provide public goods. However, governments also use tax revenue to pay for other activities or programs and to pay the costs of operating government.

9. Distribute a copy of Visual 1 to each student and display transparency of Visual 1. Tell students, as you discuss the categories, to take notes on their handouts.

   - *Social Security, Medicare, and other retirement programs:* income support for the retired and disabled and medical care for the elderly.

   - *Law enforcement and general government expenses:* federal court activities, federal law enforcement and prisons; and the general costs of the federal government including the collection of taxes and the costs of Congress.

   - *Social Programs:* medical care for the poor (Medicaid), food stamps, and income support for families with children.

- *Net Interest on the Debt:* money in the form of interest that the federal government must pay for money borrowed. **Interest** is a charge for using others' money. When we borrow money we pay the lender the amount we borrowed plus interest. When someone borrows money from us they pay back what they borrowed plus interest. When the federal government spends more than the revenue it collects, the government borrows and is charged interest.

- *National Defense:* spending for planes, tanks, and other military equipment and to pay our armed forces. This category also includes some spending to help other countries such as Egypt, Israel, and Russia.

- *Physical, Human, and Community Development:* programs for agriculture, transportation, natural resources and the environment, direct assistance to college students, and job training programs.

10. Ask students to rank the categories from largest to smallest portion of the federal budget and to record the rankings on their handout. (Strips on board may be helpful.)

11. Divide the class into groups. Distribute at least one calculator to each group and a copy of Activity 1 to each student. Read the directions and sample calculations with the students. Instruct students to complete the table.

12. Display transparency of Visual 2. Discuss:
    - Were you surprised by the results you calculated? (Answers will vary.)
    - Did your ranking from step 10 agree with the calculations?

13. Divide the class into groups and give each group 100 pennies. Instruct students to use the pennies to create a bar graph showing the portion of each federal tax dollar spent on the various categories.

14. As a class, brainstorm a list of federal expenditures from which students or their families benefit. Write the list on the board and discuss. For example:

    - highway system: The highway system benefits people whether they drive or not because goods can be moved more quickly from place to place.
    - school lunch program: Students benefit when the government provides certain foods for school.
    - free lunch program: Students who can't afford lunch are provided one.
    - national park: the beauty of the land is maintained and many individuals can engage in recreation at the park.
    - Medicare: The health of an older family member is maintained.
    - student loan: Someone unable to afford college can receive the benefits of an education.

    Note: Students may name goods or programs that are provided by state and local government tax revenue. Please point out that these are not provided by the federal government.

15. Discuss:

    - Which of the things you've listed are public goods (characterized by shared consumption and nonexclusion)? (Highway system, national park, national defense, dams, bridges.)
    - Which of the things you've listed are not public goods (aren't characterized by shared consumption and nonexclusion)? (School lunch program, Medicare, student loans.)

CLOSURE

1. Review the following:
    - What are public goods?
    - What are taxes?
    - What different types of public goods does the federal government provide?
    - What other activities does the federal

government pay for with tax revenue? Why?

EVALUATION

1. Distribute a copy of Activity 2 and a protractor to each student. Instruct them to work in their groups to complete the circle graph and to describe the similarities and differences among the *Tell-Tale Table*, penny-bar graph, and the circle graph. (All three represent the same data in a different format.)

2. Instruct students to take their circle graphs home and discuss the graph with a household member. Instruct them to ask the person to help select a category and explain how the student or the family benefits from the program, public good, or activity.

3. Ask each student to think of three examples of public goods provided by state or local government that they or their families use and explain how they benefit. (Remind students that public goods are characterized by nonexclusion and shared consumption.)

4. Ask students to explain why public goods aren't produced by private businesses.

EXTENSION

1. Use Lesson 11, *Where Does the Money Come From?* from this unit for a discussion of federal tax revenues.

2. Read *No Promises in the Wind* by Irene Hunt (New York: Berkley Books, 1986). Instruct students to research government programs developed as part of the New Deal. Using their research, students write an editorial, draw an editorial cartoon, or prepare a brief speech in favor of or in opposition to the program.

3. Read *Good-bye My Wishing Star* by Vicki Grove (New York: Scholastic, Inc., 1989), and discuss federal farm subsidy pro-

grams as related to Jens' family. Use the complementary lesson from *Economics and Children's Literature* (St. Louis: SPEC Publishers, Inc., 1993).

4. Show Video 1, "The Whiskey Rebellion," from *Taxes in U.S. History* and use the lessons provided in the teacher guide (New York: National Council on Economic Education, Agency for Instructional Technology, and the Internal Revenue Service, 1989).

5. Discuss the opportunity cost/trade-offs of changes in government taxation and spending. For example:

If the government wishes to increase spending on social programs, it must reduce spending in other areas or increase taxes to cover the cost of additional social programs.

Name _____

ACTIVITY 1
PLAY MONEY

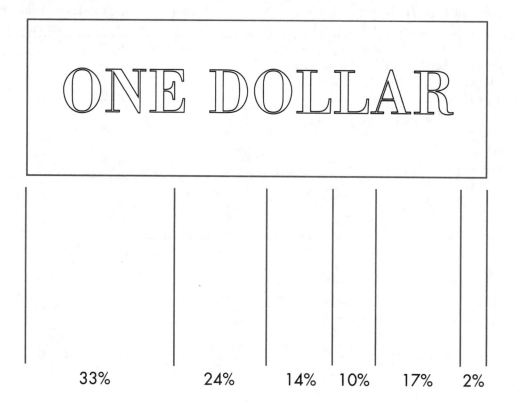

33%   24%   14%   10%   17%   2%

VISUAL 1
WHERE DOES THE FEDERAL DOLLAR GO?

1. **SOCIAL SECURITY, MEDICARE, AND OTHER RETIREMENT PROGRAMS**

2. **LAW ENFORCEMENT AND GENERAL GOVERNMENT EXPENSES**

3. **SOCIAL PROGRAMS**

4. **NET INTEREST ON THE DEBT**

5. **NATIONAL DEFENSE**

6. **PHYSICAL, HUMAN, AND COMMUNITY DEVELOPMENT**

ACTIVITY 1
TELL-TALE TABLE

Directions: Column 1 of the table below shows categories of Federal spending for 1992. The total listed at the bottom of column 2 is $1420.2 billion—that's $1,420,200,000,000! Where did this money go and what do we have to show for it? Using the procedure in the example, complete the table.

Example: Social Security, Medicare, and other Retirement

> Column 3: To calculate the portion of total outlays spent on Social Security, Medicare, and other Retirement, divide $469.7 (figure in column 2) by $1420.2 (total federal spending).
>
> Column 4: To convert .33 (figure in column 3) from a decimal to percent, multiply by 100.
>
> Column 5: To calculate the portion of a circle (degrees) represented by Social Security, Medicare, and other Retirement, multiply .33 (figure in column 3) by 360. Round to the nearest whole number.

A TELL-TALE TABLE

1 Spending Category	2 $ Spent (Billions)	3 $ Spent ÷ 1,420.2	4 %	5 Degrees
Social Security, Medicare, and other Retirement	469.7			
National Defense	348.6			
Net Interest on the Debt	199.4			
Physical, Human, and Community Developement	139.5			
Social Programs	235.6			
Law Enforcement and General Government	27.4			
TOTAL	1,420.2			

VISUAL 2
Answers
A TELL-TALE TABLE

1 SPENDING CATEGORY	2 $ Spent (Billions)	3 $ Spent ÷ 1,420.2	4 %	5 Degrees
Social Security, Medicare, and other Retirement	469.7	.33	33	119
National Defense	348.6	.24	24	86
Net Interest on the Debt	199.4	.14	14	50
Physical, Human, and Community Developement	139.5	.10	10	36
Social Programs	235.6	.17	17	61
Law Enforcement and General Government	27.4	.02	2	7
TOTAL	1,420.2	1.00	100	360 (359)

EDUCATION RESOURCE CENTER
UNIVERSITY OF DELAWARE

Name _____

ACTIVITY 2
FEDERAL SPENDING CIRCLE GRAPH

Directions: Using the information from the *Tell-Tale Table* and a protractor, construct a circle graph (pie chart).

Step 1: Place the center of the protractor on the center of the circle, making sure the line on the protractor is over the radius marked on the circle.

Step 2: Measure 119 degrees and place a mark on the circumference. Draw a radius from this point to the center of the circle.

Step 3: Label this segment "Social Security, Medicare, and other Retirement 33%."

Step 4: Place the center of the protractor on the center of the circle with the line on the protractor over the new radius.

Step 5: Measure 86 degrees and place a mark on the circumference. Draw a radius from this point to the center of the circle.

Step 6: Label this segment "National Defense 24%."

Step 7: For Net Interest on the Debt, draw a new radius 50 degrees beyond the 86 degree mark.

Step 8: Label this segment "Net Interest on the Debt 14%."

Step 9: Repeat this process for the remaining spending categories.

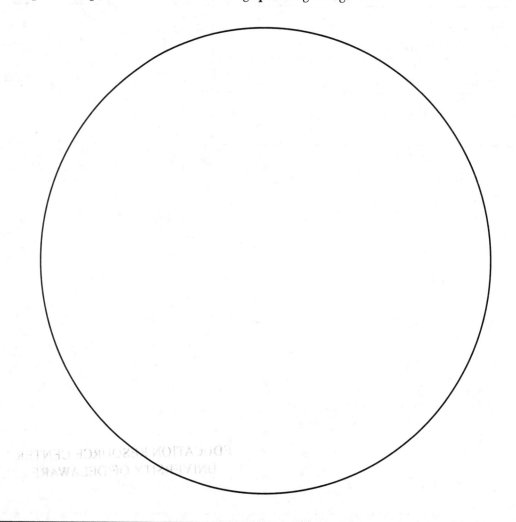

From *Focus: Middle School Economics,* © National Council on Economic Education, New York, NY

WHERE DOES THE MONEY COME FROM?

INTRODUCTION

With very few exceptions, such as revenue from the sale of public lands, the Federal Government does not have an "income" to spend on the provision of goods and services. The money used for Federal spending programs must be collected as Federal taxes or borrowed. This lesson provides students with information about the costs of government programs. This information is necessary if students are to make responsible decisions in their roles as citizens.

ECONOMIC CONCEPTS

Taxes
Categories of federal taxes
Excise taxes
Payroll taxes

RELATED CONTENT AREAS

Language arts
Mathematics

OBJECTIVES

◆ Explain that tax revenues are collected from households and businesses for use by various levels of government—federal, state, and local.

◆ Predict the types of taxes they (or their household) will have to pay over the next several years.

LESSON DESCRIPTION

Students look at the categories of federal taxation, discuss them, and calculate the percentage of total taxes collected in each category.

TIME REQUIRED

◆ Two class periods

MATERIALS

★ Activity 1, *Taxing Situations*, cut apart
★ Activity 2/Visual 1, *Who Pays Federal Taxes?*, and Visual 2, *A Table of Taxes: Answers* for each student
★ Activity 3, *A Table of Taxes*, and Activity 4, *Federal Taxes Circle Graph*, for each student
Calculator for each group
Protractor for each student

PROCEDURE

1. Explain that taxes shift resources from the private sector to the public sector to pay for the goods, services, and government operations that we, through our representatives, ask government to provide.

2. Give the following example.
   • The federal government builds post offices. To do this, the government uses tax revenue to hire workers and buy tools, equipment, and supplies. As a result, these workers, tools, equipment, and supplies are not used to construct private housing.

3. Explain that taxes are also collected at the local and state level and used to pay for goods, services, and government operations.

4. Ask students if they are aware of a good or service that is provided by state or local government. (roads, schools, parks) Discuss:
   • What things are used to produce and maintain a local park? (Land, workers, vehicles, equipment.)
   • For what private production may these resources be used? (Golf course, amusement park, landscaping company.)

5. Divide the class into groups. Distribute one of the eight cards from Activity 1 to each group. Read the following family data to the students.

★ all students—basic course material   □ average and above average students   ○ average and below average students

Family Data:
Grandmother: A teacher
Mom: Owns a convenience store
Son: Fred, age 17, student
Daughter: Maria, age 12, student

6. Instruct students, working in groups, to compute the family members' taxes based on the information in each of the situations.

7. Record student responses, making corrections if necessary:

Answers to Activity 1
1. $750.00
2. $4,500.00
3. $1.13 (Total), $0.58 (state), $0.55 (federal)
4. $16,000; $1,224
5. $48.00 (federal), $24.48 (payroll), $9.60 (state)
6. $162.50
7. $119,000
8. $0.67

8. Ask students if they are surprised by the many types of taxes this family pays. (Answers will vary.)

9. Reinforce the idea that goods and services provided by the government are not free. Taxes are imposed on households and businesses to pay for these goods, services, and the general costs of government.

10. Emphasize that federal taxes can be grouped into certain categories. These categories can help us identify who pays for the things that we, through our representatives, ask government to provide.

11. Distribute a copy of Activity 2/Visual 1 to each student and display transparency of Activity 2/Visual 1. Suggest that as you discuss the categories, students take notes on their handouts.

- **Personal income taxes:** taxes on the income earned by households and certain businesses (unincorporated). Most households pay between 15%

and 35% of their income to the federal government in personal income taxes. People with higher incomes pay the higher rates.

- **Corporate income taxes:** taxes on a business corporation's profits. Define profit as the difference between revenues (price × quantity sold) and the costs of producing or selling a good or service. Profit is a return for risk-taking. Most corporations pay a tax rate of about 34%.

- **Payroll taxes:** these include all social security and Medicare taxes. Both the employer and the employee must pay a payroll tax of 7.65% on the first $55,500 of an employee's annual earnings.

- **Excise and other miscellaneous taxes:** excise taxes are taxes you pay when you purchase a specific good, such as gasoline. Excise taxes are often included in the price of the product. The business collects the taxes and passes them on to the appropriate level of government.

12. Ask students to rank the categories from largest to smallest in terms of total federal tax receipts. Record responses.

CLOSURE

1. Divide the class into groups. Distribute at least one calculator to each group and a copy of Activity 3 to each student. Read the directions and sample calculations with the students. Instruct students to complete the table.

2. Display transparency of Visual 2. Discuss:
   - Were you surprised by the results you calculated? (Answers will vary.)
   - Did the class ranking agree with the calculations? (Answers will vary.)

3. Draw students' attention to each of the four major categories of federal taxes in Activity 2/Visual 1. Ask students who pays.

- Personal income taxes (individuals and families that earn income as defined by the government).

- Corporate income taxes (businesses that have gone through the legal process of incorporating).

- Payroll taxes (businesses and workers).

- Excise and other miscellaneous taxes (consumers of the items taxed, for example, gasoline, tobacco, alcohol, and some imported goods).

EVALUATION

1. Distribute a copy of Activity 4 and a pro-tractor to each student. Instruct them to work in their groups to complete the circle graph. Have groups describe the similarities and differences between the *Table of Taxes* and the circle graph (both represent the same data in a different format).

2. Instruct students to write a short story, "A Taxing Day In the Life of _____ ." The story should be about the various taxes paid by the student or a household member on a given day. Instruct students to be as specific as possible and to indicate if the taxes are federal taxes or those of another level of government.

3. Students should write a persuasive letter to their U.S. senator or representative supporting or opposing one of the examples of Federal taxes.

EXTENSION

1. Use Lesson 10: *Where does the Money Go?*

2. Show Video 3, "Fairness and the Income Tax, 1909," from *Taxes in U.S. History*, and use the lessons from the teacher's guide (New York: National Council on Economic Education, Agency for Instructional Technology, and Internal Revenue Service, 1992).

3. Instruct students to keep a "tax" journal for a week. In the journal they should enter items their household purchases and the amount of tax paid.

4. Instruct students to call or visit local gas stations to find out what the total tax is on a gallon of gasoline in their area. (Local gas station owners may not know.) Instruct students to ask at least three other people (family members, neighbors, and so on) if they know how much in taxes they pay on gasoline. Discuss responses.

5. Invite an Internal Revenue Service tax-payer education specialist to speak to the class. Make copies of the W-4 form and the 1040EZ form. Assist students in completing these forms.

6. Invite a local or state government member to class to discuss state and local tax rates and expenditures.

7. Contact the state revenue department for tax data in a recent year. Instruct students to use the data to construct a state revenue table and pie chart.

ACTIVITY 1
SOME TAXING SITUATIONS

1. Mom opens the mail and finds a notice from the county government indicating that one-half of the family's $1,500 property tax is due. This tax is based on the value of their home.

   What does the family owe the county now?

2. Grandmother receives a statement from her employer, Murphy Middle School. This statement, called a "W-2 Form," shows that she earned $30,000 last year in taxable income.

   If the federal income tax rate for this income level is 15%, what is the total amount of federal tax taken out of grandmother's pay?

3. Maria mows lawns in the neighborhood to earn extra money during the summer. On Saturday she buys three gallons of gas at $1.09 a gallon. "I'd make a lot more this summer if I didn't have to pay so much for gas," Maria complains to her mom. "I've got news for you, over one third of the price of a gallon of gas is excise taxes!" says Mom. "You pay 19.3 cents in state taxes and 18.4 cents in federal taxes for each gallon. Perhaps you should complain about the cost of government instead."

   What are the total taxes Maria paid on her three gallons of gas?

4. Mom pays Linda, a worker at the convenience store, $8.00 an hour. Linda works 40 hours a week and works 50 weeks of the year.

   How much does Mom pay Linda in a year? Mom must also pay a social security tax (payroll tax) of 7.65% of Linda's wages. (**Note:** Mom must pay payroll taxes for all her employees.)

   What is the total payroll tax Mom pays to the federal government based on Linda's wages?

ACTIVITY 1 (continued)

5. Linda, a full time worker at Mom's Convenience Store remembers how surprised she was when she picked up her first paycheck. Instead of the $320 check she was expecting for 40 hours of work at $8.00 an hour, she received one for $238. Then she remembered her economics class. She was a "worker" now and workers pay taxes. She had paid 15% in federal income taxes, 7.65% in social security taxes (payroll), and a flat 3% in state income taxes. These taxes had been taken out or "withheld" from the $320 she had earned.

   Find the exact amounts Linda paid in federal income taxes, payroll taxes, and state income taxes.

6. Fred finally saved $500 to make a down-payment on a used car costing $2,500 from the local dealership. His grandmother agreed to help him with a loan to finance the rest of the purchase price. Fred is excited as he drives his very own car to the Department of Motor Vehicles to apply for a license plate. His excitement fades when the clerk tells him he must pay a 6.5% state sales tax on the $2,500 purchase price. Oh no. Sales tax. He hadn't thought about that. He should have paid more attention in economics class.

   When Fred calls his mom from the Department of Motor Vehicles, how much money will he tell her he needs? (Assume he has no money with him.)

7. Mom's convenience store earned $350,000 in profits last year. Since her store operates as a small corporation, she must pay the corporate tax rate of 34% for federal corporate income taxes.

   How much does Mom owe to the federal government in taxes on the corporate profits from the store?

8. Grandmother recently quit smoking cigarettes. She wants Mom to stop selling cigarettes at the convenience store since so many students from Murphy Middle School frequent the store. "And besides," she tells Mom, "all you're doing is collecting taxes for the government, you don't make that much on each pack!"

   The price of a pack of cigarettes is $1.87. If 23% of the price represents state excise tax and 13% of the price represents federal excise tax, what is the amount (in cents) of total taxes on a pack of cigarettes?

ACTIVITY 2/VISUAL 1
WHO PAYS FEDERAL TAXES?

1. **Personal Income Taxes**

2. **Corporate Income Taxes**

3. **Payroll (Social Security) Taxes**

4. **Excise and Other Miscellaneous Taxes**

Name _____
ACTIVITY 3
A TABLE OF TAXES

Directions: Column 1 of the table below shows categories of federal tax collections. At the bottom of column 2 is $1,090 billion—that's $1,090,000,000,000 (or more than a trillion dollars)! Where does this money come from? Who pays federal taxes? Using the procedure in the example, complete the table. Use the information in columns 4 and 5 to construct a circle graph (pie chart).

Example: Personal Income Taxes

Column 3: To calculate the portion of total tax receipts that comes from personal income taxes, divide $476 (figure in column 2) by $1,090 (total federal tax receipts)

Column 4: To convert .44 (figure in column 3 from a decimal to percent, multiply by 100).

Column 5: To calculate to the portion of a circle (degrees) represented by personal income tax receipts multiply .44 (figure in column 3) by 360. Round to the nearest whole number.

A TABLE OF TAXES

1 Federal Tax Receipts Category	2 $ Collected (Billions)	3 $ Collected divided by 1,090	4 %	5 Degrees
Personal Income Taxes	476.0			
Corporated Income Taxes	100.3			
Payroll Taxes	413.7			
Excise and Other Miscellaneous Taxes	100.6			
Total	1,090.6			

VISUAL 2
Answers
A TABLE OF TAXES

1 Federal Tax Receipts Category	2 $ Collected (Billions)	3 $ Collected divided by 1,090	4 %	5 Degrees
Personal Income Taxes	476.0	.44	44	158
Corporated Income Taxes	100.3	.09	9	32
Payroll Taxes	413.7	.38	38	137
Excise and Other Miscellaneous Taxes	100.6	.09	9	32
Total	1,090.6			360 (359)

Name _____
ACTIVITY 4
FEDERAL TAXES CIRCLE GRAPH

Directions: Using the information from *A Table of Taxes* and a protractor, construct a circle graph (pie chart).

Step 1: Place the center of the protractor on the center of the circle, making sure the line on the protractor is over the radius marked on the circle.

Step 2: Measure 158 degrees and place a mark on the circumference. Draw a radius from this point to the center of the circle.

Step 3: Label this segment, "Personal Income Taxes—44%."

Step 4: Place the center of the protractor on the center of the circle with the line on the protractor over the new radius.

Step 5: Measure 32 degrees and place a mark on the circumference. Draw a radius from this point to the center of the circle.

Step 6: Label this segment, "Corporate Income Taxes—9%."

Step 7: Repeat this process for the remaining tax categories.

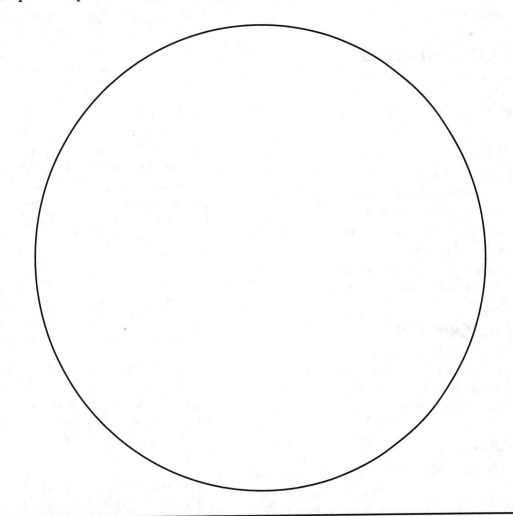

WHAT DOES THE NATION CONSUME?

INTRODUCTION

Gross domestic product (GDP) is a basic measure of national economic output. GDP is the value, expressed in dollars, of all final goods and services produced in an economy in a given year. In the United States, goods and services produced for household consumption account for approximately two-thirds of this total output.

ECONOMIC CONCEPTS

Gross domestic product
Intermediate goods
Final goods
Durables
Nondurables
Consumer spending

RELATED CONTENT AREAS

Language arts (writing and interpreting charts)
Mathematics

OBJECTIVES

♦ Define gross domestic product as the value, expressed in dollars, of all final goods and services produced in a year.

♦ Explain the difference between intermediate and final goods.

♦ Categorize consumer spending as durables, nondurables, or services.

LESSON DESCRIPTION

Students look at their consumption of goods and services in a day. Then, they consider household spending for the nation as a portion of Gross Domestic Product.

TIME REQUIRED

♦ Two class periods

MATERIALS

Visual 1, *What Does Our Nation Consume*
3 index cards per group

PROCEDURE

1. Write "Gross Domestic Product" (GDP) on the board and define as the value, expressed in dollars, of all final goods and services produced in a year.

2. Explain that what the economy produces is what is available for consumption, investment, and government spending.

3. Discuss:
   • What are goods? (Things we can use, touch, and see.)
   • What are services? (Activities people do for us.)

4. Explain that the production of these goods and services provide jobs for people in the economy. The income people earn is then used to consume goods and services.

5. Explain that final goods are goods and services sold to consumers. Intermediate goods are things that are produced and then used up in the production of other goods and services. For example, the denim produced in mills is used up in the production of jeans. Denim is an intermediate good and the jeans are a final good.

6. Ask for other examples of intermediate and final goods. (Steel in automobiles, flour in muffins, thread in a shirt, screws in a machine, wood in a table.)

7. Write, $6,400,000,000,000 ($6.4 trillion) on the board. Explain that this was the current dollar value of all the final goods and services produced in the U.S. in 1993. This is what economists call GDP.

8. Explain that we can learn more about GDP figures by looking at GDP data

collected by the Department of Commerce and the Bureau of Economic Analysis.

9. Divide class into groups of three or four. Explain that they are going to study the types of goods and services that make up a large part of the $6.4 trillion GDP.

10. Ask students, working in groups, to make a list of all the final goods and services they used from the time they woke up yesterday until they went to bed last night. Explain that each member of the group should "walk through" a typical day and then group members should combine information to create a group list. Items should not be listed more than once.

11. Ask one member from each group to report their list. As items are reported, record them on the board. Instruct a member of each group to cross items off the group's list as they are mentioned by other groups. This will help avoid repetition.

12. After recording group responses, ask students to consider items that might have been overlooked. For example, discuss:

    • How was breakfast prepared? (Microwave, toaster, refrigerator.)

    • Did you turn on the light in the bathroom to shower? (electricity) Did you use soap, shampoo, toothbrush, toothpaste?

13. Ask students to look over the list and reflect on the large number of goods and services they rely on to satisfy their wants each day. Point out several goods or services produced by businesses (CD, bread, bicycle repair). Discuss:

    • Who buys these items and activities produced by businesses? (Households, family members, consumers.)

    • How does your family obtain most of the goods and services it wants? (purchases them)

14. Explain that spending by households is called consumption or consumer spending because the products provide direct satisfaction to consumers. Emphasize that when we measure GDP, consumer spending represents the largest category. Spending for consumer goods and services makes up approximately two-thirds of all spending.

15. Write "durables" on the board and ask students what they think it means. Explain that in GDP, durables refers to a consumer good that will last longer than three years. Ask students for examples. (Bike, CD player, hockey stick.)

16. Explain that "nondurables" are consumer goods expected to last less than three years. Ask students for examples. (Hamburger, soda, shoes.)

17. Remind students that services are activities people do for us.

18. Distribute three index cards to each group. Instruct students to write "D" (durable) on one index card, "ND" (nondurable) on another, and "S" (service) on the third.

19. Explain that you will point to the items listed on the board one at a time. Each group should decide whether the item is a durable good, a nondurable good, or a service; and a member of the group should hold up the correct card.

20. As students hold up cards, record responses next to the item on the board. Note and discuss any differences among group responses.

21. Display Visual 1: *What Does Our Nation Consume?* Allow time to discuss differences between the list on the board and the visual.

22. Instruct students, working in pairs, to write four complete sentences about the table in Visual 1. For example:

    • We spent a greater percentage on services in 1993 than we did in 1963.

- Toys are nondurable goods.
- Restaurant meals are counted as nondurable goods and not services.

23. Encourage students to draw conclusions from the table about how consumer spending patterns have changed.

CLOSURE

1. Review the following:
   - What is Gross Domestic Product?
   - What are final goods?
   - What are intermediate goods?
   - What are durable goods?
   - What are nondurable goods?

EVALUATION

1. Ask each student to write "A Day in My Life as a Consumer," outlining his or her consumption of goods and services for the day.

2. Ask students, as a group, to create a GDP Consumption Collage. They may draw pictures or cut them out of newspapers and magazines. They must include examples of durable goods, nondurable goods, and services.

3. Ask students to create a visual representation of the information found in Visual 1. (Pie chart, bar graph, and so on.)

4. Instruct each group to develop a game that reviews the information they've learned in this lesson. Allow groups to trade games and play.

EXTENSION

1. Ask students to select one character from a book they are currently reading and develop a spending table for that character. The table should have durable, nondurable, and service categories.

2. Consumption figures in dollars for each year are listed in the table that follows. Instruct students, using the percentages from the table, to calculate the dollar amount of spending in each major category (durable goods, nondurable goods, services) for each year.

Year	Total Consumption (Billions of Dollars)
1963	384.1
1973	848.1
1983	2,257.5
1993	4,390.6

3. Use Lesson 13, *An Island Economy* for further information on gross domestic product.

VISUAL 1
WHAT DOES OUR NATION CONSUME? DURABLES, NONDURABLES, AND SERVICES*

	Percent of Total Consumption			
	1963	1973	1983	1993
Durable goods	13	15	12	12
Motor vehicles and parts	6	7	5	5
Furniture and household equipment (appliances, china, quilts, video and computing equipment, musical instruments, tools)	5	6	5	5
Other (jewelry, watches, books, sports and photographic equipment, boats, pleasure aircraft)	2	2	2	2
Nondurable goods	44	40	39	31
Food and beverage (includes groceries and restaurant meals)	23	21	19	15
Clothing and shoes	7	7	6	5
Gasoline and oil	3	3	4	2
Other (medicines, toiletries, cleaning products, magazines and newspapers, stationery, flowers, toys, fuel oil, tobacco products, and coal)	11	9	9	9
Services	42	45	52	57
Housing	15	14	15	14
Household operation (utilities telephone, repair and miscallaneous, services, others)	6	6	7	6
Transportation (auto repair, leasing, parking, tolls, insurance, taxi, rail, bus, airlines	3	4	4	4
Medical care (physicians, dentist, other professionals, hospitals, and nursing homes, health insurance)	6	8	12	15
Other (personal services, personal business, recreation)	12	13	13	18

*Source: Economic Report of the President. February 1994, p.286

AN ISLAND ECONOMY

INTRODUCTION

GDP (gross domestic product) measures the total output of final goods and services produced in the economy in a given year. To understand how economists measure and analyze GDP, students focus on the major components of GDP: Consumption, Investment, government expenditure, and net exports.

ECONOMIC CONCEPTS

Gross domestic product
Consumer goods
Investment
Government expenditure
Exports
Imports

RELATED CONTENT AREAS

Language arts

OBJECTIVES

- Define gross domestic product as the value, expressed in dollars, of all final goods and service produced in a year.
- Define a final good as one that will not be further processed.
- Define consumer goods and services as output produced to satisfy households.
- Explain the different categories that make up investment—capital, construction, and inventory.
- Define the government component of GDP as goods and services produced or purchased for use by all levels of the government.
- Explain the difference between exports and imports.

TIME REQUIRED

- Two class periods

LESSON DESCRIPTION

Students participate in a "readers' theater" play to learn about gross domestic product.

MATERIALS

★ Activity 1, *An Island Economy* for each student.
  Dictionaries
★ Activity 2, *Island Output* for each student.
  Props and costumes for Play (optional):
    Table, chairs, hand-made dishes, coconuts, etc.

PROCEDURE

1. Explain that students will participate in a play about seven very different people stranded on a desert island. List the cast members on the boat. (Captain, Billionaire, Celebrity, Engineer, College Professor, Student 1, Student 2.)

2. Ask the students what kinds of skills and education they think each of these people might have. Encourage responses.

3. Assign parts or write cast members on slips of paper and have students draw to assign parts. Give each student a copy of Activity 1 to read in class or for homework.

   Note: This is a "readers' theater." Students should not be required to memorize parts.

4. After the parts have been assigned and the play has been read, encourage the students to select names for each of the roles. Remember to discourage gender stereotypes when choosing names. Consider using costumes and props to build interest.

5. Divide students into pairs. Instruct pairs to use dictionaries to define sentry, foresight, provisions, inventory, wharf, macroeconomic, and derive.

6. Distribute copies of Activity 2 to each student. Explain that the play will

demonstrate a macroeconomic concept: Gross Domestic Product (GDP). Macro-economics looks at the economy as a whole and GDP measures the entire output, in dollars, of final goods and services produced in an economy in a given year. By studying the output of a simple island economy we will learn how economists measure and analyze the U.S. GDP of over $6,000,000,000,000 ($6 trillion).

7. Ask students to look at Activity 2, *Island Output*. Review the definition of GDP.

8. Explain that GDP may be broken down into four categories. Use the handout to discuss the kinds of goods and services included in the major components of GDP.

9. Since most students have read books or seen programs and movies about castaways, encourage a brief discussion about the kinds of goods and services that might be produced on a desert island. Record possibilities on the board.

10. Encourage students to listen actively and take notes on the handout during the play. Emphasize that the entire class is to respond to those parts labeled All/Castaways.

11. Present the play.

12. After the play, divide the students into small groups to share their answers.

13. Write "consumer goods" on the board. Ask *each* group to report one of the consumer goods produced on the island. Continue until all of the consumer goods are recorded on the board. Repeat this procedure, with each group adding one example, until each category (and examples) have been listed.
   - Consumer goods (Turtle soup, candles, coconut cake, guava jelly, well,* bamboo furniture, hammocks, golf equipment, caddie services.)
   - Investment goods

Capital goods (Tools, weapons, traps, fishing poles, well.*)

Construction (Housing: huts, supply hut.)

Inventory (Provisions in supply hut.)
   - Government (Dam, pool, weapons, traps, security/defense system, paths.)
   - Exports, Imports (None—a "closed economy.")
   - Weapons used as a capital good for hunting as well as a means of defense.

CLOSURE

1. Review the following:
   - What is the Gross Domestic Product? (A measure of the total output of final goods and services produced in the economy in a given year.)
   - Why was the Billionaire unhappy? (He felt unproductive.)
   - Were the castaways unproductive? (No, they produced goods and services that could be counted in the island's GDP.)
   - If you or a family member does something productive at home like cook a meal or fix your bike or the dishwasher, will that be counted in Gross Domestic Product? (No, the U.S. GDP is more complex than the island output. If you pay the bicycle shop to repair your bike, this would be part of GDP, doing it yourself would not.)

EVALUATION

1. Ask each student to write "Shipwrecked: How I Survived for a Year." Their stories should contain examples of goods and services they produced.

2. Ask the students to give examples of each of the categories of GDP.

3. Ask students to give examples of activities household members perform at home that would not be counted in GDP.

*May be listed under government because it is the island water supply.

EXTENSION

1. Assign or read portions of *Swiss Family Robinson* and *Robinson Crusoe*. Instruct students to listen or read for examples of productive output.

2. Watch Walt Disney's *Swiss Family Robinson* for examples of components of GDP. At the end of the movie an elaborate defense system is showcased.

3. Play a classroom version of "The Price is Right." Bring in pictures of appliances, cars, homes, and highway or government projects (new schools, etc.). Have students try to guess actual prices.

4. Instruct students to watch reruns of *Gilligan's Island* and bring in lists of components of GDP. Create a GDP chart in the classroom. Each day students can add their examples to the chart.

Name _____
ACTIVITY 1
AN ISLAND ECONOMY

Scene: All seven castaways are seated at a table where they have just finished eating. Everyone is talking and laughing as the Captain rises:

(_____) Captain:	May I please have everyone's attention for a moment?
All/Castaways:	Shhhhhhh! (All get quiet).
(_____) Captain:	Thank you. I just wanted all of you to know that, according to my calculations, it was exactly one year ago today that we were shipwrecked on the island. I thought this would be a good time for us to share our feelings about the past year and discuss our expectations.
All/Castaways:	Share! All we do is share!!!
(_____) Celebrity:	Do we have to sit in a circle to do this?
(_____) Student 1:	(Slaps his arm) Oh, I don't know, the mosquitoes are really bad out here tonight . . .
(_____) Student 2:	(Yawning) I'm tired, I was up early fishing . . .
(_____) Engineer:	Yes and I need to get an early start tomorrow on that dam if we want another fresh water pool for bathing.
(_____) College Prof:	Well, (patting hands once on table) if no one has anything to share, I suggest we all . . .
(_____) Billionaire:	(Interrupting in a sad voice) What has been most difficult for me this past year on the island has been being . . . (choke, choke) . . . (whispers) unemployed.
All/Castaways:	What?
(_____) Billionaire:	(A little louder, but still not audible) un-em-ployed.
All/Castaways:	We still can't hear you!
(_____) Billionaire:	(Stands and begins pacing) (Very loudly) UNEMPLOYED! I said unemployed! I haven't earned one paycheck in over 12 months! I used to put in 12 or 15 hour days running my companies. It was exhilarating! I worked hard and in return I got income, stock options and frequent flyer miles. I feel so, so (sighs) unproductive. (Billionaire slumps into chair.)
All/Castaways:	Ahhhh/Ahwww (Castaways offer solace, patting Billionaire on back).
(_____) College Prof:	(Rising–tapping on prop) Excuse me everyone, could I say something please? We have been many things on this island—angry, frustrated, sunburned, and sometimes even happy and satisfied. The *one* thing (looks around at crew and focuses on Billionaire) we have *not* been is unproductive.
All/Castaways:	NOT.
(_____) Captain:	The Professor is right. From that first day we washed up on the beach after the storm we have all been busy as bees from sunrise to sunset.

From *Focus: Middle School Economics*, © National Council on Economic Education, New York, NY

ACTIVITY 1 (continued)

All/Castaways:	Busy as bees, Buzzzzzzzzzzzzz.
(_____) Student 1:	(Sighing) I remember the first night when we all sat around the fire. We decided then to establish priorities and try to make our life as safe and comfortable as possible.
(_____) College Prof:	Yes, and look at how successful we have been! We have produced a commendable supply of goods and services and we are all alive!
(_____) Student 2:	You call this (looking around) "goods and services"?
All/Castaways:	Goods and services???
(_____) College Prof:	Absolutely. (Looking at Engineer and Captain) It was your ideas and skills that were crucial in developing our security system. We were not sure what kind of wildlife, or other mysteries the island might hold. The tools, weapons, and traps that you two made from the ship's wreckage provide an excellent defense system.
(_____) Engineer:	(Looking over all of the crew) And each one of you takes a regular turn on sentry duty.
(_____) Student 2:	So we *have* produced a pretty good defense system—kind of like the local police, the FBI, and the Navy Seals all rolled into one!!
(_____) Captain:	And don't forget the same tools, weapons, and traps we use for defense we also use over and over again for fishing and hunting.
(_____) Celebrity:	(Looking at nails and cuticles) Oh! Speaking of hunting and trapping, if no one has any objections, I'd like to use any animal furs we have this year for a coat or perhaps a short jacket. I don't know about the rest of you, but I really find it a bit chilly on the beach in the evenings. While I do prefer ranch mink, rabbit or otter will have to do. Is that okay with everyone?
All/Castaways:	(All turn to Celebrity) NO! (All turn back to table)
(_____) Billionaire:	Okay, okay, so we have produced a degree of safety and I guess the turtle soup and the coconut cake you two (waves hands at both students) make is pretty good . . .
(_____) Celebrity:	(Interrupting) What about my guava jelly?? I thought you liked my guava jelly?? It was your idea for me to make an extra case of it to store in the supply hut. I thought you liked it (frowning).
All/Castaways:	Don't you like the guava jelly??
(_____) Billionaire:	Yes, yes, the guava jelly is great. But jelly is no substitute for a job. (Stands and begins pacing again) Work! Measurable output! Something to show for yourself at the end of a day! Oh, how I miss that!
(_____) College Prof:	(Turns to Billionaire) Haven't you been listening??
All/Castaways:	Listen . . . Do Da Do.
(_____) College Prof:	You do work! there is measurable output! You designed and almost single-handedly built our intricate system of paths *and* all of our housing.
(_____) Engineer:	That's right! I was busy working on the well. You did everything.

ACTIVITY 1 (continued)

(_____) Student 1: And what about the supply hut? You insisted we build it and stock it with at least six months worth of provisions. You taught us all the words of your great-grandfather . . . (in a deep voice) "goods on a shelf are like money in the bank to a good business person." Because of your foresight and work, we are prepared for emergencies.

(_____) Student 2: And I see you in the supply hut every night taking inventory to make sure we have enough dried fish, coconuts, fresh water, and candles . . .

(_____) Celebrity: (Interrupting) Ah-hemm . . . and guava jelly!

(_____) Student 2: And GUAVA JELLY, so we could make it through a long storm, or a spell of poor hunting or fishing. Your contributions to our island economy are very real.

(_____) Captain: (Turning to Billionaire) So you see, you have "worked" and produced measurable output. We all have. In fact, I'm very proud of the bamboo tables and chairs I made this year.

(_____) Billionaire: (Still not convinced—quietly shaking his head)

(_____) Engineer: (Turning to Captain) Those *are* nice and comfortable. You know, if you went to Wharf One . . .

All/Castaways: Wharf one! or Wharf wharf.

(_____) Captain: The import store back home?

(_____) Engineer: Yes, at Wharf One people pay good money for the kind of furniture you made for us.

(_____) Captain: You're right! I've seen hammocks like the ones I produced there too!

(_____) College Prof: Exactly! (Turning to Billionaire) We've worked and we've produced. In fact, if we added up the value of all the final goods and services we have produced this year on our island, we could derive our very own GDP— gross domestic product!

(_____) Student 1 & 2: Uh-oh.

(_____) Student 1: (Groans) I feel an economics lecture coming on.

All/Castaways: Ahhhhhhhh (groan and grumble).

(_____) College Prof: Now wait just a minute everybody, a *small* dose of macroeconomics is just what the doctor ordered to chase away (_____ Billionaire's) case of the blues! It won't take long, all we have to do is think through our first year and make a few calculations. It will do us all some good to see what we have accomplished by measuring our gross domestic product. So what do you think? (Turning to _____ Billionaire) Will you help?

(_____) Billionaire: Let me see if I understand. (Getting excited) We are going to tally up all the goods and services we've produced this year? But I thought you needed prices to do that (voice falling), there are no price tags on anything we've produced.

(_____) College Prof: No problem! We can estimate the prices or even make a game out of it like the TV program, what is it . . . the "Right Price"? We were just talk-

	ing about the furniture prices at Wharf One. I'm sure we can do it.
(_____) Student 1:	But I learned in economics class that GDP only measures goods and services that pass through official markets. You need buyers and sellers in order to have a market . . .
(_____) College Prof:	Yes, you're right. But remember you are consumers and producers. Remember, at home all the things we have now on the island we used to buy from businesses or they were provided by the government through our tax dollars. We may have informal markets but we do have real output.
(_____) Billionaire:	(Thoughtfully) You know, this might just work. Calculating our GDP for this year will provide a base we can use to measure and compare our growth over the coming years.
All/Castaways:	Coming years!!! What coming years???!!!
(_____) Celebrity:	Bite your tongue! There aren't going to be any "coming years." (Rising solemnly) I'm sure we will be rescued any day now. (Everyone gets quiet) My agent must be frantic with worry . . . (voice trailing off).
(_____) Captain:	(Rises, comforts _____ Celebrity—patting on back) Yes, of course, we're all hoping to go home soon . . .
All/Castaways:	(All nodding in agreement) Yea, yea, any day now.
(_____) Captain:	But until we do, this project might lift our spirits and our output. And if I understand what the Professor has been saying, hard work and more output means a higher standard of living. We all want that, don't we?
(_____) College Prof:	Absolutely.
(_____) Engineer:	You bet.
(_____) Billionaire:	Count me in!
(_____) Student 1:	For sure!
(_____) Student 2:	Sounds good to me.
(_____) Celebrity:	(Reluctantly) Well . . . I guess so, as long as we're stuck here, . . . hey, you do plan to count the golf equipment I made in this GHP you're concocting?
(_____) Student 1:	The term is GDP! And you call clam shells attached to a bamboo pole and an avocado pit golf equipment??
(_____) Celebrity	(Voice rising) I certainly can if you call what you were doing caddying!
(_____) Captain:	All right you two, now remember, act civilized please.
(_____) College Prof:	(Picking up a pad and pencil or feather/quill, looks out at audience) This may be harder than we think . . .
All/Castaways:	THE END.

ACTIVITY 2
ISLAND OUTPUT

Instructions: Listen carefully to the play *An Island Economy*. Help the Castaways to muster up their GDP for the year by answering the questions in the chart below:

Consumer Goods: Goods and services produced to satisfy households. This output includes goods like food and furniture and services such as doctors or VCR repair.	Investment Goods: (1) Tools, machines, and equipment (capital) produced for use by businesses. These "capital" goods can be used over and over like a milkshake machine at a fast-food restaurant. (2) All kinds of construction—from homes and apartments to malls and factories are also "Investment." (3) Products sitting on shelves or in warehouses waiting to be sold are the part of the investment called "inventory."
What consumer goods and services have been produced on the island?	Even though there are no "businesses" on the island, are there items produced by the crew that might otherwise be considered "investment"?

ACTIVITY 2 (continued)

Government: Goods and services produced or purchased for use by all levels of the government. This output includes military equipment for national defense, new roads and bridges, and public education.

What goods and services produced on the island would you expect to be produced by some level of government back at home?

Exports and Imports: Exports are goods and services produced in one country and sold to people in other countries. Exports are a part of our GDP. Imports are goods and services produced in one country and bought by people in another country. GDP includes net exports, which equals exports minus imports.

Will the crew have any exports to count in their GDP? Why or why not? How about imports?

NO FREE LUNCH

INTRODUCTION

In their roles as responsible citizens, students learn to consider both the costs and the benefits related to public policy issues. This lesson uses budgets and a decision tree to structure student analysis of taxing and spending issues.

ECONOMIC CONCEPTS

Budget
Taxes
Cost-benefit analysis
Trade-offs

RELATED CONTENT AREAS

Critical thinking
Language arts

OBJECTIVES

◆ Recognize the costs and benefits of goods and services provided by the government.

◆ Distinguish between tax increases and spending decreases.

◆ Identify possible trade-offs that can be made to balance a budget.

LESSON DESCRIPTION

Students use a decision tree to analyze a budget problem at a public school.

TIME REQUIRED

◆ Two class periods

MATERIALS

★ Activities 1, *A Muddle at Murphy Middle School*, and Activity 2, *Murphy Middle Decision Tree* for each student
Visual 1, *Decision Tree*

PROCEDURE

1. Walk into class carrying a large sign that says, "There is no such thing as a free lunch." Place the sign on the wall. This is a saying very popular with economists and one that is invaluable to us in our role as responsible citizens. Encourage students to discuss what they think this means. (Answers will vary.)

2. Discuss:
   - What is a school "free lunch" program? (Students who qualify do not have to bring money to school to pay for lunch.)
   - Is the lunch really free? (No, the lunches are paid for by a federal program, so taxpayers really pay for the "free" lunches.)

3. Explain that when public schools provide goods like lunches and services like education, they are not free. Tax revenue is used to pay for the costs of operating a public school. Define taxes as required payments to government imposed on households and businesses.

4. Distribute a copy of Activity 1 to each student. Read the activity as a class. Brainstorm possible solutions, listing them on the chalkboard or overhead. (Answers will vary.)

5. Explain that households, businesses, government, and even schools must have a "budget." Define "budget" as a plan to balance or coordinate revenue (or income to a household) and expenses. If Murphy Middle School wants to have a balanced budget, it can either increase its revenue or reduce its expenses (costs).

6. Using the board or overhead, have students circle the possible solutions that involve increasing revenue (increasing taxes/fund-raising) and draw a rectangle around solutions that involve decreasing expenses (dropping athletic programs, reducing services, larger class sizes).

7. Display Visual 1. Use the *Decision Tree* to evaluate the costs and benefits (pros and cons) of the two basic solutions to the budget problem at Murphy Middle School. Emphasize there is not one

"right" answer. The decision tree helps people look critically at both the costs and the benefits of spending or taxing options.

8. Divide the class into small groups. Distribute a copy of Activity 2 to each student. Assign one of the possible spending cuts or revenue enhancers listed on the board in #4 to each group and tell them to use the Decision Tree to analyze the costs and benefits for the option. Each group should reach a consensus about whether the option should be adopted by Murphy Middle School.

9. Ask one or two students from each group to report the group's decision and the factors that most influenced their decision. Record group responses. Ask students what additional information, if any, would have helped in making their decision.

CLOSURE

1. After all groups have reported, take a vote by show of hands or secret ballot to determine if Murphy Middle School should try to have taxes increased or should reduce spending. Make sure any spending reductions are very specific.

2. Discuss the election results. If the class voted to increase taxes, what will happen if the school is still unable to balance its budget, despite the tax increase? (Going to voters for a second tax increase is not likely to be successful, so spending will have to be reduced.)

3. Explain that many economic decisions are a result of trade-offs. Encourage students to think of options to the budget problem at Murphy Middle School that might involve a "trade-off." For example, could the school accept a smaller tax increase and agree to cut less popular programs?

EVALUATION

1. Students (individually or in groups) use the Decision Tree to analyze costs and benefits for a local or national issue that involves voter approval or uses public funds: examples, building a new airport, expanding a light rail system, or protecting an endangered species. (Answers may vary. Emphasize "no free lunch." Students may not approve spending programs without considering costs and how the program or project will be funded.)

2. Instruct students to write a persuasive paragraph on "Why I Think Taxes Should Not Be Increased to Balance the Budget at Murphy Middle School," or "How I Think Murphy Middle School Can Reduce Operating Costs."

3. Ask students to answer the following questions in their *Economics Role Journals* regarding the role of responsible citizen.

   • Is this one of your roles now? If so, how?

   • How will you fill this role in the future?

   • How will being a responsible citizen benefit you?

   • How is your role as decision maker related to your role as a responsible citizen?

EXTENSION

1. Instruct students to create a personal budget based on an income (take-home pay) of $800 a month. Students should do research and collect information from household members to develop a complete list of possible expenses. Students may assume they are 18 and either live at home or have their own apartment. Emphasize that the $800 a month is "fixed" so items like a $400 car payment may be tough to budget!

2. Invite a certified financial planner to speak to the class regarding budgets, saving, and spending.

3. Invite a school board member or a school district finance administrator to visit the class and discuss sources and uses of revenue for the district.

4. Use revenue information for the school or school district to construct pie charts depicting sources of revenue and costs of operation.

5. Present students with a hypothetical tax increase for the district. Ask them to develop a persuasive letter to the voters supporting or opposing the tax increase.

Name _____
ACTIVITY 1
A MUDDLE AT MURPHY MIDDLE SCHOOL

Murphy Middle School has a problem. Some federal programs the school has offered have lost funding. The school would like to continue these programs.

The school must pay for teacher salaries and benefits (including health insurance), special programs and resources to help students academically, staff and administrators' salaries and benefits, and expenses for books, supplies, food service, athletics, utilities, buses, and building maintenance. All of these costs have increased, some more than others.

The main source of tax revenue for the school is the property taxes collected by the local government. These property taxes are paid by citizens who own homes or real estate in the school district. There are also some state tax revenues and special tax revenues from the federal government that the school has come to depend on over the years. Last year the amount of tax revenue the school received from the state and from the federal government was reduced. This reduction in tax revenues together with the increasing costs of operating the school spells budget disaster.

What can the school do so that tax revenues equal or cover the costs of operating the school?

Brainstorm Notes:

VISUAL 1
DECISION TREE

Decision

BENEFITS (Pros)	BENEFITS (Pros)
1. Maintain current programs 2. Keep all teachers and staff 3. Keep same class sizes	1. Faster–no voter approval required 2. May cut unpopular or wasteful programs 3. Taxpayers' income will not be reduced
COSTS (Cons)	COSTS (Cons)
1. Voters may not approve a tax increase 2. Taxpayers will have less income and may spend and save less in the community 3. Decrease in community support because of increased taxes	1. Decrease in community support because some popular programs may be cut 2. Some teachers or staff may be let go 3. Larger class sizes

Raise Revenue
(Taxes)

Alternative

Reduce Spending

Alternative

Spending Exceeds
Tax Revenues

Problem

From *Focus: Middle School Economics*, © National Council on Economic Education, New York, NY

Name _____

ACTIVITY 2
MURPHY MIDDLE SCHOOL DECISION TREE

Decision

BENEFITS (Pros)	BENEFITS (Pros)
COST (Cons)	COST (Cons)

Choice	Choice

Problem

INTRODUCTION TO PRUDENT SAVER

This unit contains one lesson that helps students understand their roles as prudent savers in the economy.

Lesson 15 shows students that savings occur when individuals, businesses, and the economy as a whole do not consume all of current income (output). Students also learn that to a large extent, the process of saving and investment represents a division of productive resources from the output of goods and services for current consumption to the creation of up-to-date, technologically advanced capital goods that can expand production and increase the productivity of human and natural resources.

SAVERS AND BORROWERS

INTRODUCTION

Saving occurs when individuals, businesses, and the economy as a whole do not consume all of current income (or output). From an individual standpoint, saving represents income not spent. Much unspent income may be placed in financial institutions such as banks and savings and loan associations, which in turn make loans to those who wish to buy capital resources or other resources. Individuals may also place their savings more directly, by purchasing newly issued shares of corporate stock, bonds, and similar financial instruments or by buying instruments already issued from others, who may use the funds they receive to buy new issues. Individuals may also contribute to pension funds or purchase mutual funds. To a large extent, the process of saving and investment represents a diversion of productive resources from the output of goods and services for current consumption to the creation of up-to-date, technologically advanced capital goods that can expand production and increase the productivity of human and natural resources.

ECONOMIC CONCEPTS

Saving
Interest
Financial intermediaries

RELATED CONTENT AREAS

Language arts

OBJECTIVES

◆ Recognize the role of financial intermediaries in the lending/borrowing process.

◆ Define saving as income not spent.

◆ Define interest as payment for the use of money.

LESSON DESCRIPTION

In this lesson, students encounter difficulties in lending and borrowing. They identify financial institutions as effective intermediaries in this process. In closure they discuss the role credit can have on the growth of a community.

TIME REQUIRED

◆ One class period

MATERIALS

★ Activity 1, *Saver/Borrower Cards*, cut apart Visual 1, *Mrs. Altonia's Mall*, and Visual 2, *Mrs. Altonia's Mall* Flow Diagram: Answers

★ Activity 2, *Mrs. Altonia's Mall Flow Diagram*, for each pair of students

PROCEDURE

1. Discuss:

   • Have you ever saved in order to buy something in the future?

   • When you save, what do you give up? (Buying goods and services in the present.) Explain that when people save they do not spend all of their income on goods and services in the present. They reserve some income for the purchase of goods and services in the future. The present consumption of goods and services is the opportunity cost of saving.

   • Have you ever borrowed from someone to make a purchase?

   • When you borrow, what do you give up? (Purchasing goods and services in the future.) Explain that when you borrow, you use someone else's money to buy goods and services in the present. You repay the loan in the future. So, you have less money with which to purchase goods and services in the future. The future goods and/or services you give up are the opportunity cost of borrowing.

2. Distribute a Saver/Borrower Card from Activity 1 to each student and instruct students to read their cards.

3. Explain that students who have borrowed cards will try to find a person or people willing to lend them money. They should try to borrow as much as their card indicates. Those who have lender cards will try to lend money to a person or people. They should try to lend as much as their card indicates.

4. Allow 5 to 10 minutes for borrowing and lending. After the time is up, discuss the following:

   • Some of you had saved money. What were you trying to do with the savings? (Lend it out, earn interest and have the money with interest available to spend in the future.)

   • Why did some of you want to borrow money? (Wanted to make a large purchase for which they didn't have enough money; wanted to start a business and needed money for building, equipment, and merchandise or supplies.)

   • Were those of you who had money to lend able to lend as much as you wanted? Why or why not? (Found person or people willing to borrow what I had to lend and pay the interest rate I was charging or couldn't find person/people willing to borrow what I had to lend and pay the interest rate I was charging; ran out of time.)

   • As a lender, did you have other concerns? (This took a lot of time. What if the person you lent to didn't pay you back?)

   • Were the borrowers able to borrow as much money as you wanted? Why or why not? (Found a person willing to lend the amount I wanted at an interest rate I was willing to pay or could not find person/people willing to lend the amount I wanted at an interest rate I was willing to pay; ran out of time.)

   • What could make this borrowing/lending process easier? (Someone to accept lenders' money and pay them interest, then make loans to others and charge them interest.)

   • What would have helped you borrow or lend? Guide students toward the idea of an intermediary, someone to "collect" savings and make loans.

   • Do we have these kinds of intermediaries in our society? (Yes, banks, savings and loans, and other financial institutions are financial intermediaries.)

4. Explain when people have unspent income they often save it in banks or savings and loans. The banks or savings and loans pay savers interest. The banks or savings and loans lend the money to people who wish to borrow and charge the borrowers interest. So, interest is a payment for using other people's money.

5. Restate the idea that banks and savings and loans are financial intermediaries. Financial intermediaries accept deposits and make loans.

6. As a class, brainstorm a list of the qualities students would like a financial intermediary to have and reasons why these qualities would be important. (Stable, safe, convenient location, reliable, ethical.)

CLOSURE

1. Display transparency of Visual 1. Read with the class and discuss:

   • What was Mrs. Altonia's problem? (She wants to build a shopping mall but she does not have enough money.)

   • What did she do? (Borrowed the money she still needed from her bank.)

   • Why does the bank require a loan application? (To help determine whether Mrs. Altonia will be able to repay the loan.)

   • Why is the bank able to lend the money to Mrs. Altonia? (Because other people in the community have forgone current consumption and placed their savings in the bank.)

   • What do the savers receive in return? (The bank pays them interest.)

   • What is the savers' opportunity cost?

(Current consumption of goods and services.)

- Why does the bank pay interest? (The bank is paying to use someone else's money.)

- Why does the bank charge Mrs. Altonia interest? (Mrs. Altonia is paying to use someone else's money.)

- What is Mrs. Altonia's opportunity cost? (Future consumption of goods and services.)

- What impact will a new shopping mall have on the community? (List student ideas on the board: new places to buy goods and services; construction jobs to build the mall, jobs at the stores and shops when the mall is finished, jobs for truckers and other workers who deliver goods; loss of business for existing stores in the community; traffic congestion.)

- Who will work at the mall?

- What will these workers do with their income? (Spend now; save now and spend later.)

EVALUATION

1. Divide the class into pairs. Distribute a copy of Activity 2 to each pair and instruct them to complete the flow diagram for Altonia's Mall. Display Visual 2 and allow time for students to check their diagrams.

2. Review the following ideas through discussion.

   - Saving represents income individuals do not spend.

   - Interest is payment for the use of money.

   - Financial intermediaries accept deposits and make loans.

3. Instruct each student to write a short story about a character who wants to borrow money. The story must tell the item(s) for which the character wants to borrow, how much he or she wants to borrow, the financial institution from which he or she plans to borrow, the interest rate for the

loan, and an explanation of why the money is available for lending.

4. Ask students to answer the following questions in their *Economic Role Journals*, regarding the role of prudent saver:

   - Is this one of your roles now? If so, how?

   - How will you fill this role in the future?

   - How will being a prudent saver benefit you?

   - How is your role as a decision maker related to your role as a prudent saver?

EXTENSION

1. Have each student survey three adults regarding the items they borrow money to purchase. Combine the data for the whole class. Divide the class into groups, and instruct each group to construct a graph representing the data.

2. Read *Where the Red Fern Grows*, by Wilson Rawls (New York: Bantam Books, 1974), and use the complementary lesson in *Economics and Children's Literature* (St. Louis: SPEC Publishers, 1993).

3. Use lessons from *The Money Tree* (Federal Reserve Bank of St. Louis, 1989). The section on Money and Banks offers a number of lessons to enhance middle-school students' understanding of banks, saving, and credit.

4. Divide the class into groups. Instruct each group to research the savings and loan crisis in the 1980s. They should prepare an oral report along with at least two visuals.

5. Divide the class into small groups. Instruct students to cut out ads for various banks and savings and loans or call banks and savings and loans to determine the level of interest charged and the repayment schedule for a new car loan with a down payment of $5,000 and with no down payment. Ask the groups to develop a chart, table, or graphic comparing the information found.

ACTIVITY 1
SAVER/BORROWER CARDS - ROUND 1

You have saved $10,000 You would like to lend the money and earn at least 8% interest.	You have saved $5,000 You would like to end the money and earn at least 8% interest.
You have saved $1,000 You would like to lend the money and earn at least 8% interest.	You have saved $3,000 You would like to end the money and earn at least 8% interest.
You have saved $500 You would like to lend the money and earn at least 8% interest.	You have saved $50,000 You would like to end the money and earn at least 8% interest.
You have saved $20,000 You would like to lend the money and earn at least 8% interest.	You have saved $80,000 You would like to end the money and earn at least 8% interest.
You have saved $250 You would like to lend the money and earn at least 8% interest.	You have saved $500 You would like to end the money and earn at least 8% interest.

ACTIVITY 1 (continued)

You want to borrow $15,000 You want to pay no more than 3% interest.	You want to borrow $5,000 You want to pay no more than 3% interest.
You want to borrow $4,000 You want to pay no more than 3% interest.	You want to borrow $12,000 You want to pay no more than 3% interest.
You want to borrow $30,000 You want to pay no more than 3% interest.	You want to borrow $2,500 You want to pay no more than 3% interest.
You want to borrow $750 You want to pay no more than 3% interest.	You want to borrow $6,000 You want to pay no more than 3% interest.
You want to borrow $7,500 You want to pay no more than 3% interest.	You want to borrow $100,000 You want to pay no more than 3% interest.
You want to borrow $350 You want to pay no more than 3% interest.	

VISUAL 1
MRS. ALTONIA'S MALL

Mrs. Altonia owns and operates Altonia Construction. Her two daughters and her son are part owners in the company. The company has been in business for 15 years. Recently, Mrs. Altonia purchased 10 acres of land in a nearby community. The land is zoned for commercial use. She plans to build a shopping mall on the land. The mall will include a large department store, fifteen small shops, 2 restaurants, and parking. Altonia Construction estimates that when completed the mall will employ 3,000 people, some full time and some part time.

In order to complete the project, Mrs. Altonia had to secure an additional $600,000. She met with her bank and completed the necessary applications to obtain the loan. After carefully considering the company's application, the bank agreed to lend the company the money. The bank will be charging 7% interest on the loan.

Construction at the mall will begin in a month. In order to complete the work on schedule, Altonia Construction will be adding three additional crews.

VISUAL 1
ANSWERS
MRS. ALTONIA'S MALL—
FLOW DIAGRAM

**Savers Have
Unspent Income**

**Banks and
Other
Financial
Intermediaries**

**Loans to
Businesses
(Altonia
Construction)**

Constructions Jobs ------- **Workers
earn income**   **Save for later**

**Buy goods and
services**

Mall jobs ---------- **Workers
earn income**   **Save for later**

**Buy goods and
services**

**Loans to Businesses
(Altonia Construction)**

**Construction
Jobs**   **Mall jobs**

ACTIVITY 2
MRS. ALTONIA'S MALL—FLOW DIAGRAM

Savers Have
Unspent Income

Banks and
Other
Financial
Intermediaries

Loans to
Businesses
(Altonia
Construction)

INTRODUCTION TO GLOBAL PARTICIPANT

This unit contains two lessons that help students understand their roles as producers, consumers, and voting citizens in a global economy. Gaining perspective on their roles in the world economy will help students develop the ability to compete in the global marketplace.

Lesson 16 shows how specialization and exchange have helped our economy grow and how both have benefitted individuals both as workers and consumers. Through a look at economic production in the early days of westward expansion in the United States, students learn how the concepts of absolute and comparative advantage led settlers to specialize and trade and, in so doing, improve their economic well-being.

Lesson 17 deals with issues revolving around free trade. The lesson helps students examine the impact of trade barriers on prices and employment and to analyze which groups gain and which lose from the imposition of trade barriers such as tariffs and quotas.

FRONTIER SPECIALISTS

INTRODUCTION

The level of output in an economy can be increased through specialization. Economic specialization occurs when people produce a narrower range of goods and services than they consume. Such specialization requires people to participate in the exchange of goods and services with other people and increases interdependence. Specialization and exchange occur because of the unequal distribution of productive resources and comparative advantage—the condition that exists when one party can produce a product at a lower opportunity cost than another party. Thus, nations (or individuals) can benefit from specialization and trade even though productive resources are unevenly distributed.

ECONOMIC CONCEPTS

Specialization
Exchange
Interdependence
Absolute and comparative advantage

RELATED CONTENT AREAS

Social studies/U.S. history
Language arts
Mathematics

OBJECTIVES

◆ Identify the benefits of specialization.

◆ Explain why specialization creates interdependence.

◆ Identify absolute advantage.

◆ Calculate comparative advantage.

◆ Explain how comparative advantage leads to specialization and trade.

LESSON DESCRIPTION

Using a simulation about frontier families, this lesson helps students gain an understanding of the benefits of specialization and how comparative advantage forms the basis for exchange in a market economy.

TIME REQUIRED

◆ One class period

MATERIALS

☐ Activity 1, *Family Role Cards* for each group

☐ Activity 2, *Frontier Specialists*
Transparency of first page of Activity 2, *Frontier Specialists*

PROCEDURE

1. Divide students into groups representing two frontier families. Distribute Activity 1 role card to each family and Activity 2 to each student. Display transparency of Activity 2 and read the scenario with the class.

2. Define **absolute advantage:** A person has an absolute advantage if he or she can produce more of a product with the same amount of resources as another person. (For this simulation, assume that each family has an equal amount of land and that the production shown in the chart is for 100 hours of labor.) Discuss:

   • In which item does each family have an absolute advantage? (Sanchez: meat; Jacobson: corn)

   • Would the families be better off if each family produced only one item and traded with the others? (Yes. They could produce more total units of each item; by trading, they will each have as much or more of each item than they did before.)

   • Ask each "family" if they are willing to depend on the other family for basic necessities—food, clothing, etc.? What if Mr. Jacobson became ill and the family only produced 25 units of corn? What if the Sanchez family decides to move and no longer is near enough to provide the meat? (If either of the families does not produce fully, the others will not receive as much of that good as they want.)

Note: One of the potential disadvantages of specialization and trade is that people become interdependent. If one person is not able to produce fully, it affects those who depend on him or her.

- Do you think the Jacobsons would be willing to trade 2 units of corn to get 1 unit of meat? Does that sound like a fair "price" to the other family? (If the price varies much from this, trade might not be beneficial for both families. The "price" of trading for a family cannot be higher than the opportunity cost of producing all items for themselves.)

3. Put the following production schedule on the chalkboard or overhead and tell students: The Jacobsons have moved. A new family, the Martins, now live near the Sanchez farm. The two families are interested in trading cloth and meat. The Sanchez family is better at both (they have an absolute advantage in the production of both cloth and meat):

	Cloth	Meat
Sanchez	5	10
Martin	4	6

4. Ask students if the Sanchez family can still benefit from trading? (Students are likely to answer no, since the Sanchez family is better at producing both items.)

5. Define **comparative advantage:** One party has a comparative advantage if they can produce a product at a lower opportunity cost than another party. To see if both families will benefit, students must see what each family would give up—the "cost" of one item in terms of the other item. The "cost" of one item in terms of the other is found by calculating the ratio between the two items. (The ratio of meat to cloth for Sanchez: 2:1; for Martin 1.5:1.)

6. Explain that for a family to produce one additional unit of meat, they must give up producing some cloth. Have students calculate the opportunity cost of producing one additional unit of meat for each family.

Discuss:

- How much cloth would the Sanchez family give up to produce one additional unit of meat? The Martins? (For the Sanchez family to produce one additional unit of meat, they would have to give up a half unit of cloth. For the Martin family to produce an additional unit of meat, they would have to give up two-thirds unit of cloth.) Which family has a comparative advantage in meat (has to give up the least cloth)? (Sanchez)

- How much meat would the Sanchez family give up to produce one additional unit of cloth? The Martins? (The Sanchez family would give up 2 units of meat; the Martin would give up 1.5 units of meat.) Which family has a comparative advantage in cloth? (Martin)

CLOSURE

1. Should the two families specialize and trade? Which should produce cloth and which should produce meat? (It would benefit both families to specialize and trade. If the Sanchez family produces all meat, they can produce a total of 20 units of meat. If the Martin produce all cloth, they can produce a total of 9 units of cloth. Total production for the two families increases and they will be better off.)

2. Can you think of any reasons the families might decide not to trade, even though they could produce more by specializing? (If they specialize and trade, the families become interdependent. If something happens so that one family cannot produce all of the item in which they specialize, it will affect the other family as well.)

3. Review these concepts:
   - Specialization benefits consumers because it makes more choices available at a lower cost.
   - Interdependence results from specialization; societies today are very interdependent.
   - Absolute advantage means that one party (individual, nation, and so on) can produce more of a product than another party with the same resources.
   - Comparative advantage means that one party can produce a product at a lower opportunity cost than another. Comparative advantage is a primary basis for specialization and trade.

EVALUATION

1. Provide students with the following information and instruct them to answer the questions: Mrs. Sanchez can weave a yard of cloth in 3 hours; she can plow an acre of land in 2 hours. Mr. Sanchez can weave a yard of cloth in 5 hours; he can plow an acre of land in 2.5 hours. Mrs. Sanchez is better at both. Should she do all the work? If they specialize, which job should each do?

   - What is the cost in acres of land for Mrs. Sanchez to weave a yard of cloth? (1.5 acres)
   - What is the cost in yards of cloth for Mrs. Sanchez to plow one acre of land? (2/3 yard)
   - What is the cost in acres of land for Mr. Sanchez to weave a yard of cloth? (2 acres)
   - What is the cost in yards of cloth for Mr. Sanchez to plow an acre of land? (1/2 yard)

   (Mrs. Sanchez should weave and Mr. Sanchez should plow. A yard of cloth costs Mr. Sanchez 2 acres of plowing; it only costs Mrs. Sanchez 1.5 acres of plowing.)

2. Discuss: Citrus fruits are grown in Florida and California, cattle are raised in Montana and Wyoming, and corn covers the fields of Illinois and Iowa. Yet, we know that cattle can be raised in Florida, and corn can be grown in California. Why do states/regions specialize?

   (The United States has vast resources which are distributed unevenly throughout regions. Because resources differ from region to region, specialization has developed. Even though cattle can be raised in Florida, Florida has a comparative advantage in citrus fruit and is better off specializing in that. The same holds true for other regions.)

3. Using a product map (from social studies texts or similar resources), have students identify how states or regions specialize. Discuss:
   - What has led to regional specialization? (Climate, natural resources, availability of transportation, human resources, and so on.)
   - What products do you use that are made in other regions of the United States or in other countries? (Answers will vary.) Discuss the benefits we receive from specialization and trade:

     —more products to choose from

     —lower prices due to increased competition among producers

EXTENSION

1. After doing research, have the students develop a product map showing regional specialization in the United States.

2. Have students select a country or a region of the United States and write a report on the products or services in which those regions specialize. The report should include reasons for specialization in those products.

3. Have students identify examples of specialization in the school (cooks, teachers, administrators, custodial staff, clerical staff) or have them ask their parents about specialization at their place of employment.

4. Read *Mountain Born* by Elizabeth Yates (New York: Walker & Company, 1993), and use the corresponding lessons from *Economics and Children's Literature* (St. Louis: SPEC Publishers, 1993).

5. Use *The International News Journal, Inc.* (New York: National Council on Economic Education, 1992), to teach about the United States and its trade relationships with seven other countries.

6. Select a familiar product. Instruct students to list the inputs used to produce the product. Ask students to use reference books to find the state or country from which the inputs come. Have the students locate the place where the product is produced and the source of the inputs. Mark the locations on a map. Then have students connect the locations with yarn to demonstrate interdependence.

Name _____
ACTIVITY 1
FAMILY ROLE CARDS

THE SANCHEZ FAMILY

Family members:

Mr. Sanchez: came to the U.S. from Mexico. An excellent hunter; provides ample meat for the family, as well as hides and fur for clothing and other uses. Also raises some corn on the land, although their land is not very fertile.

Mrs. Sanchez: helps raise corn as well as keeping a small garden and some fruit trees. Collects wild berries in the woods. Has a hand loom for weaving cloth, a very slow process.

Children: Jose, Maria, and Cortez, ages 15, 10, and 2. Jose helps with hunting, chores, and gardening; Maria helps take care of Cortez.

THE JACOBSON FAMILY

Family members:

Mr. Jacobson: raised on a farm in Sweden. Has excellent land and is a good farmer. Grows corn primarily.

Mrs. Jacobson: helps Mr. Jacobson with the farming. Cares for the children. Keeps a small garden.

Children: Angelica, Martin, and Philip, ages 16, 14, and 3. All help with chores and with the farming and garden.

Name _____

ACTIVITY 2
FRONTIER SPECIALISTS

Use the following information to answer the questions:

The year is 1840. Your family moved one year ago to a sparsely populated area west of the Mississippi River. Only one other family lives within 10 miles of the house you have built. It is 50 miles to the nearest town. Each family has 50 acres of land.

Each family has been producing all its own food and clothing for the past year. Families generally keep to themselves except when they meet each week for worship at one of the homes. As they have come to know each other, Mr. Sanchez notices that each family seems to have some special skills and resources. The Jacobsons seem to have an absolute advantage in growing corn. And the Sanchez family an absolute advantage in hunting meat.

Food Production Without Specialization: (units)

Family	Corn	Meat
Sanchez	8	10
Jacobson	35	6
TOTAL	43	16

The families meet to exchange information to see if they would be better off if each specialized in what they did best and exchanged the extra they produced for other items they need. Here is what they found. (Assume each family has an equal amount of land and that the production shown represents 100 hours of labor.):

Food Production With Specialization: (units)

Family	Corn	Meat
Sanchez	0	20
Jacobson	50	0
TOTAL	50	20

ACTIVITY 2 (continued)

1. In which item does each family have an absolute advantage?

_____

_____

_____

_____

_____

2. Would the families be better off if each family produced only one item and traded with the others? Why or why not?

_____

_____

_____

_____

_____

3. What will happen if one of the families does not produce all it can?

_____

_____

_____

_____

_____

_____

_____

_____

DON'T FENCE ME OUT! (BARRIERS TO TRADE)

INTRODUCTION

The concept of comparative advantage makes a strong case for free, unrestricted trade between nations. Yet, some people support the use of tariffs or quotas to restrict or stop the flow of goods and services among countries. These barriers to trade exist in most countries and have differing effects on producers and consumers in the countries involved.

ECONOMIC CONCEPTS

Free trade
Barriers to trade
Quota
Tariff
Export subsidy
Product standard

RELATED CONTENT AREAS

Social studies (history, government)
Language arts

OBJECTIVES

◆ Identify and describe commonly used trade barriers.

◆ Explain why trade barriers are imposed.

◆ Predict the impact of trade barriers on prices.

◆ Analyze which groups gain and which groups lose from the imposition of trade barriers.

LESSON DESCRIPTION

Students explore the impact of various barriers to trade and determine who gains and who loses when trade barriers are imposed.

TIME REQUIRED

◆ 3–4 class periods

Note to the Teacher: The arguments for and against trade restrictions involve social and political issues as well as the arguments of economic efficiency. Therefore, as students debate the issue in the lesson activities, there are not always right and wrong answers. If jobs in an inefficient domestic industry are being protected by trade barriers, there are costs to that decision—less long-term growth, higher prices, inefficient use of resources, etc. These are costs many people fail to recognize when trade issues are discussed. Both with and without trade barriers, there are gainers and losers.

MATERIALS

Buy American sign
Visual 1, *Who Is It?*
★ Activity 1, *Barriers to Trade.* Activity 2, *Barriers to Trade:* Answers, and Activity 4, *The Trail of the Trade Tariff* for each student
★ Activity 3, *Barriers Role Cards* for each group
Small balance scale and six small weights of equal size for each group
★ Activity 5, *A Sweet Deal* (Role 1 for half the class and Role 2 for the other half)

PROCEDURE

1. A few days prior to teaching this lesson post a sign saying *Buy American* but do not discuss it.

2. Ask students why they agree or disagree with the slogan *Buy American* (Answers will vary; some may support barriers because they feel it protects jobs; some may feel it is patriotic to buy American-made goods; some may say U.S. quality is better or worse than foreign quality, etc.)

3. Have the students examine the clothes they are wearing and other items they own to determine where these items were produced. Generate a list on the overhead or chalkboard. Discuss:

   • How do you benefit from being able to buy goods made in other countries? (More choices; lower prices.)

- Would you favor a policy that would raise the price on T-shirts and reduce the amount available? (Answers will likely be negative.)

4. Explain that even though economists believe free trade will be mutually beneficial for living standards in countries that trade with each other, many barriers to trade exist today. Most barriers raise prices and reduce choice. Show Visual 1, with answers (right column) covered. Ask students what country is Country A? Country B? Country C? (Answers will vary.)

5. Uncover the answers in right column. Ask if students are surprised by any of these answers. Explain that even though the answers given are correct, many other country names would also have been correct. Almost all countries impose some barriers to trade.

6. Ask students why they think countries establish policies that restrict trade? (Answers include to protect homeland industries or new industries, to protect jobs, to gain income for the government.) If students are not able to come up with answers, be sure to note these reasons. If necessary, use examples from history. (Example: The early colonies placed tariffs on British goods to let the new industries in this country get a good start. In the 1970s, unions and U.S. automobile manufacturers supported quotas on less expensive imported cars to help keep their own products competitive. U.S. steel manufacturers objected to Japan providing subsidies to their steel firms that made steel imported into the U.S. less expensive than domestic steel.)

7. Distribute a copy of Activity 1 to each student. Read the handout with the class, noting reasons for establishing trade barriers. Ask the students to predict what the impact of each policy might be on consumers and workers in the country that imposes the barriers. Provide examples of each type of trade barrier:

Tariff: U.S. places excise taxes on imported leather goods. This increases the cost of imported wallets and purses leading to higher prices for consumers in U.S.; this helps maintain jobs at competing U.S. firms (in the short term).

Quotas: U.S. establishes a quota on cars imported from Japan. This reduces total supply of cars which increases prices on both imported and domestic cars for consumers. This may protect jobs for workers in U.S. automobile firms (in the short term). This increases profits for U.S. firms.

Note: Voluntary export restraints for imported cars was the option of choice for the U.S. in the 1980s.

Export Subsidy: Government of Country A provides a subsidy through tax breaks to tractor producing firms in their country. This allows the firms to sell their tractors at lower prices thus competing well in both their country and other countries. Consumers benefit from lower prices, but citizens (consumers) in Country A are paying for the subsidy through their taxes.

Product Standards: Safety requirements, product features, and packaging requirements vary from country to country. Meeting these standards increases the cost of producing products for export to many different countries and thereby makes the products more expensive to the consumer. This also reduces choice.

8. Divide the class into 6 groups. Distribute a Barriers Role Card from Activity 3. Have a balance and six small weights of equal size at the front of the room. Instruct someone from each group to read the group's role card to the class.

9. Distribute a copy of Activity 4 to each student. Explain that they will analyze the impact of a proposed tariff on CD players imported into the United States. Provide the following instructions:

- As a group, answer the questions on your role card.

- Select one member of the group as spokesperson. This person will remain in the group's area to meet with representatives from other groups.

- Send the remaining group members to other groups as representatives. They should find out how a tariff will affect the group(s) they visit. (Some representatives may have to visit two groups.)

- Using all the information representatives have learned, decide who gains and who loses with the establishment of a tariff. Be prepared to explain why a group gains or loses. Record your answers on the *Trail of Trade Tariff* activity.

- Share results from all groups.

- As each group is identified as a gainer or loser, place a weight on the balance. If the group gains, place the weight on the left side of the scale. If the group loses, place the weight on the right side of the scale.

10. Allow time for group work.

- **Note:** Order of groups on the trails is not important; gainers and losers should be assigned to the correct trail.

CLOSURE

1. Discuss:

- Which people or groups will gain by the imposition of a tariff on imported CD players? Why? [Magna Electronics Corporation (higher sales and profits), workers for Magna (maintain job, at least in the short run), Mintronics owner (better chance to compete and become established in the industry).]

- Which people or groups will lose by the imposition of the tariff? Why? [CD company in Xland (fewer sales due to higher price), workers at Xland firm (less being sold, may get laid off), U.S. consumers (paying higher prices for CD players than if more competition were allowed; reduces consumer choices).]

- Are there other people or groups that would be affected? In what way? (Consumers in Xland, stockholders of firms, people in related industries, governments in communities where impacted firms pay taxes, unemployed people in both countries, etc.; impacts will vary.)

- Are there other trade barriers that might be used? (Quotas, standards, export subsidies are all possible.) How would they affect each group? (Quotas and product standards would have an impact similar to tariffs; export subsidies would help consumers in other countries who buy our exports, but U.S. taxpayers would pay for the subsidies.)

- Is a tariff fair? Why or why not? (Answers will vary; remind them of their answers to the question at the beginning of this lesson about a policy that would raise the price of T-shirts.) Does Mintronics need protection more than Magna? (Some may feel so, since it is a new firm.) What if Magna and Mintronics both export a lot of their product to Xland and Xland decides to impose a 25% tariff? (Note that this is how "trade wars" start; in the long run, tariffs have a negative affect on all people involved.)

2. Have students identify what kind of barrier is being imposed in each of these cases:

- A tax of 15% makes jewelry from Mexico more expensive than jewelry made in the United States. (tariff)

- Korea may export only 15,000 automobiles a year to the United States. (quota)

- The rungs on the ladder of any bulldozer sold in Germany must be 12 inches apart, but U.S. manufacturers generally make the rungs 15 inches apart. (product standards)

- A new textile firm asks its government to provide financial assistance to make it possible to sell its products overseas at a lower price that will compete well in other countries. (export subsidy)

EVALUATION

1. Distribute copies of Student Activity 5 (Role 1 to half the class and Role 2 to the other half.). Read through instructions with the students. After completing the work, have students report their results through a "Session of the House." Papers may also be collected for evaluation.

2. Have each student select a product that is imported into the United States as well as manufactured in the United States (or has been in the past). Students should create a flowchart with two sides, showing all the people affected by a tariff or quota on the item. One side of the flow should show people affected negatively, the other side should show those who gain from the protective measure. Remind students to think of the impact on firms, workers, and consumers of related products—complements and substitutes. Example: United States places a tariff on imported cocoa.

EXTENSION

1. Ask students to answer the following questions in their *Economics Role Journal* regarding the role of global participant.
   - Is this one of your roles now? If so, how?
   - How will you fill this role in the future?
   - How will being a global participant benefit you?
   - How is your role as decision maker related to being a global participant?

2. If Productive Worker: Lesson One, "The T-Rrific T's Company: Production Decisions," from this guide has been used, have students create flowcharts that would show the impact of a tariff, a quota, and an export subsidy on T-Rrific T's and all related parties. Or have them write a letter to their representative in Congress on behalf of T-Rrific T's arguing for or against a trade barrier on imported T-shirts.

3. Use Lesson 2, "The Protective Tariff Issue, 1832" from *Taxes in U.S. History,* (New York: National Council on Economic Education, Agency for Instructional Technology, and the Internal Revenue Service 1992) to teach about a tariff issue in United States history.

Positive Impact		Negative Impact	
Firms Producing Cocoa Substitutes	← U.S. Cocoa Producers	South American Cocoa Producers →	South American Workers
Workers ←	Cocoa →	U.S. Chocolate Candy Makers →	Firms producing complements
Communities where firms pay taxes		U.S. candy consumers →	Workers

4. Use lessons from Unit 3, "Trade Barriers" from *Master Curriculum Guide in Economics, Teaching Strategies: International Trade* (New York: National Council on Economic Education, 1988).

5. Read *A Pocketful of Goobers: A Story about George Washington Carver* by Barbara Mitchell; see lesson from *Economics and Children's Literature* SPEC Publishers, (St. Louis: 1993).

6. Use lessons from *The International News Journal, Inc.* (New York: National Council on Economic Education, 1992), to teach about United States trade relations with seven other countries.

7. Use the list of items and countries generated in procedure step #3 to create a country/item bar graph for the class.

8. Use Lesson 11, *Where Does the Money Come From?* from this guide. This lesson deals with various taxes.

VISUAL 1
WHO IS IT?

COUNTRY A   **United States**

Restricts number of cars that
may be imported each year
from Country X

COUNTRY B   **Japan**

Provides subsidies to some
companies so they can sell their
products at lower prices to
other countries

COUNTRY C   **United States**

Imposes taxes on certain
imported goods

Name _____
ACTIVITY 1
BARRIERS TO TRADE

Definitions:

Barriers to Trade: Policies that restrict the free flow of goods and services between countries; types commonly used are tariffs, quotas, export subsidies, and standards.

Tariff: Tax on imported goods or services; a tariff may be used to raise revenues for the government imposing the tariff, but is more commonly used to reduce consumption by domestic consumers of the imported good or service. A tariff increases the price of an imported good, thus making the good less attractive to consumers than a less expensive domestic good.

Quota: Limit on the amount of an imported good allowed into the country during a given period of time (i.e., one year); a quota reduces not only the amount of imported goods available but also the total amount of that good available; when supply is decreased, price increases for the consumer; thus, a quota, like a tariff, raises the prices of the good for consumers.

Export Subsidy: Government financial assistance to a firm that allows a firm to sell its product at a reduced price; this makes the product more competitive when exported to other countries. Consumers (both at home and abroad) benefit from lower prices but the subsidy is paid for by taxpayers in the country providing the subsidy.

Product Standards: A type of "hidden" trade barrier; most countries set their own standards for product safety, content, packaging, etc.; if a standard for a product differs in Country A from the standards of Country B, firms in Country B will spend additional money in production to meet the standards of Country A if they want to export their product there; this addition to the cost of production will make their product more expensive for consumers in Country A to buy and will encourage consumers there to buy domestic (Country A) products instead. Consumers in Country A will pay higher prices for these goods than they would without a trade barrier.

Questions for Discussion

1. With each type of trade barrier, who is affected?

2. How does each policy affect prices and jobs?

Name _____

ACTIVITY 2
BARRIERS TO TRADE: ANSWERS

Definitions:

Barriers to Trade: Policies that restrict the free flow of goods and services between countries; types commonly used are tariffs, quotas, export subsidies, and standards.

Tariff: Tax on imported goods or services; a tariff may be used to raise revenues for the government imposing the tariff, but is more commonly used to reduce consumption by domestic consumers of the imported good or service. A tariff increases the price of an imported good, thus making the good less attractive to consumers than a less expensive domestic good.

Quota: Limit on the amount of an imported good allowed into the country during a given period of time (i.e., one year); a quota reduces not only the amount of imported goods available but also the total amount of that good available; when supply is decreased, price increases for the consumer; thus, a quota, like a tariff, raises the prices of the good for consumers.

Export Subsidy: Government financial assistance to a firm that allows a firm to sell its product at a reduced price; this makes the product more competitive when exported to other countries. Consumers (both at home and abroad) benefit from lower prices but the subsidy is paid for by taxpayers in the country providing the subsidy.

Product Standards: A type of "hidden" trade barrier; most countries set their own standards for product safety, content, packaging, etc.; if a standard for a product differs in Country A from the standards of Country B, firms in Country B will spend additional money in production to meet the standards of Country A if they want to export their product there; this addition to the cost of production will make their product more expensive in Country A to buy and will encourage consumers there to buy domestic (Country A) products instead. Consumers in Country A will pay higher prices for these goods than they would without a trade barrier.

Questions for Discussion

1. With each type of trade barrier, who is affected?

   Corporations in both countries; consumers and workers in both countries; stockholders; competing firms; firms producing related products; taxpayers; governments; etc.

2. How does each policy affect prices and jobs?

   Most policies increase the price of goods both because of increased costs and because they restrict supply; reductions in supply can also decrease employment; a subsidy may reduce prices, by placing a burden on taxpayers.

Name _____

ACTIVITY 3
BARRIERS ROLE CARDS

PRODUCER OF CD PLAYERS IN XLAND

You are a producer of CD players in Xland. You can make your product at a cost that allows you to sell a CD player for $189 (U.S.). You export many CD players to the U.S.

1. What will the price be for your CD player in the United States with the tariff?

2. How does the tariff affect your company and workers?

MANAGEMENT OF MAGNA ELECTRONICS CORPORATION

Your firm is the largest producer of CD players in the United States. You can make your product at a cost that allows you to sell a CD player for $195 (U.S.). Your main competition in this market is from the company in Xland who can sell their CD player for $189 (U.S.) without any tariff.

1. How will the tariff affect your firm's profits and your workers?

2. Do you support the tariff? Why or why not?

TEENAGE CONSUMERS IN UNITED STATES

You are a teenage consumer in the United States. When you go to buy a new CD player, both the Magna (price $195) and the Xland (price $226) have the features you want. The tariff on imports makes the Xland product cost more than the Magna product. You have a limited budget and did not want to spend over $200.

1. Which product would you buy? Why?

2. How does the tariff affect you?

Name _____
ACTIVITY 3 (continued)

WORKER AT MAGNA ELECTRONICS CORPORATION

You are a worker at Magna Electronics Corporation, the largest manufacturer of CD players in the United States. The company's main competitor is a company from Xland that exports many CDs to the United States. If your company does not keep up its present sales level, you will be laid off from work.

1. How will the tariff on CD players affect you?

2. Do you support the tariff on CD players? Why or why not?

OWNER OF MINTRONICS, INC.

You are the owner of Mintronics, Inc., a new U.S. firm producing CD players. Being a small, new company, your production costs are rather high, making the price of your CD players $200 (U.S.).

1. How will the tariff on CD players affect your company?

2. Do you support the tariff on CD players? Why or why not?

PRODUCER OF COMPACT DISCS

You are the producer of compact discs in the United States. Your sales depend on the sales of CD players to U.S. consumers. The lower the price of CD players, the more consumers will buy of the players and of your discs. Your discs play equally well on either domestic or foreign CD players.

1. How will the tariff on CD players affect your firm?

2. Do you support the tariff on CD players? Why or why not?

Name _____

ACTIVITY 4
THE TRAIL OF THE TRADE TARIFF

Instructions:

1. As a group, read your role and answer the questions on your card.

2. Exchange information with each of the other groups to see how a tariff will affect them.

3. Decide who gains and who loses with the establishment of a tariff. Be prepared to explain why a group gains or loses. Record your answers on the *Trail of the Trade Tariff* below.

4. Share your results with the whole class. As each group is identified as a gainer or loser, place a weight on the balance. If the group gains, place the weight on the left side of the scale. If the group loses, place the weight on the right side of the scale.

TARIFF POLICY: The U.S. government has placed a 20% tariff on compact disc players imported for sale here.

TRAIL OF THE TRADE TARIFF

Loser's Trail	Gainer's Trail

ACTIVITY 5
A SWEET DEAL

Role 1
**You are a member of Congress representing a district
with many growers of sugar cane.**

Congress is debating a House Bill that proposes placing a tariff on all imported sugar. This tariff would raise the price of imported sugar in the United States by 10%. You are meeting with other representatives from districts similar to yours to discuss this proposed tariff.

Another group of Representatives come from areas with firms that produce candy and other products using sugar. They will be debating you on the floor of the House.

Prepare your arguments for or against the tariff proposal. Use the space below to outline your position. Be sure to consider ALL people that will be affected by a tariff. Remember, you represent sugar growers but you also represent consumers.

After completing discussion, you will report your results through a "session of the House."

Role 2
**You are a member of Congress representing a district
with many firms that produce candy or other products using sugar.**

Congress is debating a House Bill that proposes placing a tariff on all imported sugar. This tariff would raise the price of imported sugar in the United States by 10%. You are meeting with other representatives from districts similar to yours to discuss this proposed tariff.

Another group of Representatives come from areas with many growers of sugar cane. They will be debating you on the floor of the House.

Prepare your arguments for or against the tariff proposal. Use the space below to outline your position. Be sure to consider ALL people that will be affected by a tariff. Remember, you represent candy firms but you also represent consumers.

After completing discussion, you will report your results through a "session of the House."

ROLE CALL QUIZ

INTRODUCTION

As they participate in the economic system, members of society have a number of common and overlapping roles. This lesson reviews the six broad role categories: productive worker, responsible citizen, knowledgeable consumer, lifelong decision maker, prudent saver, and global participant, and introduces a simple model of a market economic system.

An economic system is the institutional framework that a society uses to allocate its resources to produce and distribute goods and services. In a predominantly market economic system, the major decisions about production and distribution are made in a decentralized manner by individual households and business firms. A circular flow model is a way of illustrating the operation of a market economic system.

This lesson is the culminating activity. Success depends upon students having mastered most of the concepts taught through the other lessons in the program.

ECONOMIC CONCEPTS

Economic system
Circular flow

RELATED CONTENT AREAS

Language arts
Critical thinking

OBJECTIVES

◆ Define economic system.
◆ Review economic content from previous lessons.
◆ Construct circular flow model.
◆ Review roles people have in the economy.

LESSON DESCRIPTION

Students play a game to review the roles and economic content about which they have learned. They use information to construct a circular flow model of the economy.

TIME REQUIRED

◆ Two class periods

MATERIALS

Tape
6 5″ × 8″ index cards with one of the following written on each card: prudent saver, knowledgeable consumer, productive worker, lifelong decision maker, citizen, global participant
★ Activity 1, *Economic Role Call Quiz Questions* cut apart
30 5″ × 8″ index cards with a Role Call Quiz Question taped to one side and the point value written on the other side.
A container in which small pieces of paper with numbers representing the number of teams in the class have been placed.
★ Activity 2, *Score Sheet* for each group
☐ Activity 3 *The Circular Flow*
One set of circular flow cards from Activity 4
11″ × 14″ piece of paper, pencil, and clear tape for each pair of students
Visual 1, *Circular Flow Diagram*

PROCEDURE

1. Prior to teaching the lesson, prepare the *Economic Role Call* cards as explained in the materials section.

2. Construct a "Jeopardy" style game board on the chalkboard. To do this, tape the category cards on the board to create six category columns. Tape the question cards on the board under the appropriate columns with the point value facing out.

3. Divide the class into teams of three. Allow each team to select a number from the container. Instruct them to choose a spokesperson and a scorekeeper for their group. As questions are asked, the group will have 30 seconds to decide whether to answer or pass the question to the next group. The spokesperson will have to report the group's decision.

4. Distribute a copy of Activity 2, *Score Sheet* to each group. Explain that the

scorekeeper must record the gain or loss of points with each question.

5. Explain teams will be playing *Economic Role Call Quiz*. Groups will be asked to answer questions. If they answer correctly, they will receive the number of points indicated on the question card and may continue their turn. If they answer incorrectly, they lose the number of points indicated on the card and their turn passes to the next group in numerical order. If they do not know the answer, they may pass the question to the next group. If the second group answers correctly, that group receives double the assigned points and continues by selecting the next question. If they do not answer, they may pass the question and avoid losing points.

6. Begin by reading a question to group 1. After 30 seconds is up, ask the spokesperson to give the group's answer or pass the question to the next group. Each question card has a point value for a correct answer. If appropriate, the scorekeeper should record the group's points.

7. Continue playing until all question cards have been used. Instruct scorekeepers to total points. Provide prizes for students in the winning group and, if possible, smaller items to recognize all players.

CLOSURE

1. Write the term **economic system** on the board. Ask students if they can explain what an economic system is. (An economic system is the framework that a society uses to allocate its resources to produce and distribute goods and services.)

2. Explain that students have learned a lot about the economic system and people's roles in the economic system. They are going to use their knowledge to create a model of our economic system.

3. Divide the class into pairs. Distribute a set of circular flow cards from Activity

4, a copy of Activity 3, a sheet of 11″ × 14″ paper, a pencil, and clear tape to each pair of students.

4. Instruct students, based on the information read, to place the cards in a circle with *Goods and Services Market* card at twelve o'clock on the circle, *Business Owners* card at three o'clock, *Resources Market* card at six o'clock, and *Individuals and Families* card at nine o'clock.

5. Display transparency of Visual 1 and discuss:
   - What group provides resources? (families and individuals) Instruct students to draw an arrow from the families and individuals box to the resource market box as you draw an arrow on the transparency. Label the arrow "supply resources."
   - What group uses resources? (businesses) Instruct students to draw an arrow from the resource market to the businesses and label the arrow "use resources."
   - What do businesses do with these resources? (produce goods and services) Instruct students to draw an arrow from the businesses to the market for goods and services and label the arrow "supply goods and services."
   - Who uses goods and services? (families and individuals) Instruct students to draw an arrow from the market for goods and services to families and individuals and label the arrow "use goods and services."
   - What do families and individuals receive in return for providing resources in the market? (income) Instruct students to draw an arrow from the resource market box to the families and individuals box as you draw and label it "earn income."
   - On what do families spend their income? (Purchasing goods and services.) Instruct students to draw an arrow from families and individuals to market for goods and services and

label the arrow "spend income."

- What do businesses receive in return for the goods and services they supply? (revenue) Instruct students to draw an arrow from the market for goods and services to businesses and label the arrow "receive revenue."

- What must businesses pay for with their revenue? (Pay for resources or pay for costs of production.) Instruct students to draw an arrow from the businesses to market for resources and label the arrow "pay for costs of production."

7. Ask students to compare their completed diagram to your transparency. Discuss:

- What is different from the two? (In some cases students have the circular flow cards in different places.)

- What is similar about the two? (The market cards are always across from each other; the families and individuals card and the business card are always across from each other; one set of arrows moves in one direction and the other set in the opposite direction.)

8. Explain that the arrows describing the movement of goods, services, and resources make up the "real" flow in the circular flow. The arrows describing the movement of money payments make up the "money" flow.

9. Discuss:

- In what roles do people participate as individuals and members of households? (Worker, consumer, citizen, global participant, saver, decision maker.)

- In what roles do people participate as members of businesses? (Worker, citizen, decision maker, global participant.)

10. Ask students to record these roles on the lines provided on the circular flow models.

EVALUATION

1. Conduct the webbing activity from the introductory lesson in this strategies guide again. Place the same students in each group. Compare each group's original webs with the new web for inclusion of economic terms, connections reflecting role overlap, and connections to the economic system.

2. Ask students to write an essay describing how they think people's roles will change in ten years. The following can be used as starter sentences.

- What technological developments might change how you purchase goods and services?

- What job do you expect to have and what technological developments might change how you perform your job?

- In which of the six roles will you be more involved in the future?

EXTENSION

1. Instruct students to work in groups and prepare an economics review box. The boxes should be decorated to represent economics and should include five student-developed games (matching, memory, etc.) and/or puzzles (logic, crossword, word search, etc.) that review the economics students have learned through the lessons in this unit. After the boxes are complete, groups should trade boxes and play the games and solve the puzzles found in the new box.

2. Choose a role and write a poem describing the attributes of that role.

3. Have groups in the class develop puppets and a play to teach younger students a basic economic concept(s) (goods, services, decision making, opportunity cost, production).

4. Make arrangements for students to conduct puppet shows at a neighboring elementary school.

ACTIVITY 1
ECONOMIC ROLE CALL QUIZ QUESTIONS

KNOWLEDGEABLE CONSUMERS

1. Give an example of something you purchase that is good. (1 point)

2. Give an example of something you purchase that is a service. (2 points)

3. Why is a mail-order catalog an example of a market? (3 points)

4. If the price of candy bars increases what will happen to the quantity consumers will buy? (4 points)

5. If the price of popcorn at the movies goes up, what will happen in the market for sodas at the movies? (5 points)

6. Last year the rate of inflation was 5%. Your allowance did not increase. What happened to your purchasing power? (4 points)

LIFELONG DECISION MAKERS

1. This evening your baseball team has a game at 6:00 p.m. However, tryouts for the under 13 fall soccer team are also being held at 6:00 p.m. If you choose to attend soccer tryouts, what is your opportunity cost? (1 point)

2. You received $50 for your birthday. You've decided to buy either new wheels for your roller blades or a new video game. You can use the game all year long, your parents allow you to play video games, the game is fun but you can only play with one other person, and if you play the video game you won't be outside with other friends. With new wheels on your roller blades, you will be able to play street hockey after school with friends during nice weather, roller hockey is good exercise, your parents allow you to play roller hockey but they worry about injuries. If you choose to buy the video game, what is a resulting trade-off? (3 points)

PRODUCTIVE WORKERS

1. A new computer can help employees do their work in half the time it takes without the computer. What economic concept does this illustrate? (1 point)

2. New machinery can help a firm produce their products in half the time it takes without the machinery. How does this benefit the firm? Its employees? Stockholders? Consumers? Community? (**Note:** Could use different groups in different rounds of the game.) (3 points)

3. The price of sugar goes up. How will sugar producers react? (3 points)

4. The price of leather goes up. What will happen in the market for leather athletic shoes? (2 points)

ACTIVITY 1 (continued)

5. A firm can sell 2,000 basketballs at $15.00 each or 1,200 basketballs at $20.00 each. It costs $12.00 to make each ball. At which price will the firm make the most profit? (4 points)

6. Pierre wants to increase his profits at the bakery. Will increasing his prices on all products help him increase his profit? Explain your answer. (3 points)

RESPONSIBLE CITIZEN

1. Why is flood control along a river an example of a public good? (2 points)

2. What are taxes? Name a type of tax your family pays. (2 points)

3. Provide an example of a nondurable good that you purchase. (1 point)

4. Consumer goods make up one component of gross domestic product. What is another component? (2 points)

5. When analyzing a policy it is important to consider the pros and cons of each option. What is another term for pros and cons? (3 points)

PRUDENT SAVER

1. What is interest? (1 point)

GLOBAL PARTICIPANT

1. Even though orange trees will grow in the state of Illinois, farmers there choose to grow crops such as wheat, soybeans, and corn? Why? (2 points)

2. How does specialization and trade benefit consumers? (1 point)

3. The U.S. government levies an excise tax on leather goods imported from other countries. What is the impact of this tax on U.S. consumers of leather goods? (3 points)

4. You are a sugar farmer in Central America. How do you feel about U.S. excise taxes on the
   1. Even though orange trees will grow in the state of Illinois, farmers there choose to grow crops such as wheat, soybeans, and corn? Why? (2 points)

2. How does specialization and trade benefit consumers? (1 point)

3. The U.S. government levies an excise tax on leather goods imported from other countries. What is the impact of this tax on U.S. consumers of leather goods? (3 points)

4. You are a sugar farmer in Central America. How do you feel about U.S. excise taxes on the sugar you ship to the United States?

ACTIVITY 2
SCORE SHEET

Question Number	Points Won or Lost
_____	_____
_____	_____
_____	_____
_____	_____
_____	_____
_____	_____
_____	_____
_____	_____
_____	_____
_____	_____
_____	_____

TOTAL POINTS _____

Name _____
ACTIVITY 3
THE CIRCULAR FLOW

One way to show how an economic system works is with a model or diagram. The operation of a market economy can be shown with a circle model. Use the information below along with the paper, cards, and pencils you've been given to construct such a model.

1. The resource market provides a way for resources to be bought and sold.

2. The goods and services market provides a way for goods and services to be bought and sold.

3. Individuals and families own resources. These include human, natural, and capital resources. Individuals and families provide resources and receive income in exchange. They use the income to buy goods and services in the goods and services market.

4. Businesses buy from the resources market. Businesses use the rseources to produce goods and services. They sell the goods and services and use the revenue they receive to pay families and individuals for the use of resources.

Individuals and Families (Resource Owners)	Goods & Services Market
Business Owners	Resources Market

ACTIVITY 1: Answers
ECONOMIC ROLE CALL QUIZ QUESTIONS

KNOWLEDGEABLE CONSUMERS

1. Give an example of something you purchase that is a good. (1 point) (Answers will vary.)

2. Give an example of something you purchase that is a service. (2 points) (Answers will vary.)

3. Why is a mail-order catalog an example of a market? (3 points) (Buyers and sellers interact, goods and services available.)

4. If the price of candy bars increases, what will happen to the quantity consumers will buy? (4 points) (Quantity demanded will decrease.)

5. If the price of popcorn at the movies goes up, what will happen in the market for sodas at the movies? (5 points) (Demand for sodas will decrease.)

6. Last year the rate of inflation was 5%. Your allowance did not increase. What happened to your purchasing power? (4 points) (decreased)

LIFELONG DECISION MAKERS

1. This evening your baseball team has a game at 6:00 p.m. However, tryouts for the under 13 fall soccer team are also being held at 6:00 p.m. If you choose to attend soccer tryouts, what is your opportunity cost? (1 point) (Playing in the baseball game.)

2. You received $50 for your birthday. You've decided to buy either new wheels for your roller blades or a new video game. You can use the game all year long, your parents allow you to play video games, the game is fun but you can only play with one other person, and if you play the video game you won't be outside with other friends. With new wheels on your roller blades, you will be able to play street hockey after school with friends during nice weather, roller hockey is good exercise, your parents allow you to play roller hockey but they worry about injuries. If you choose to buy the video game, what is a resulting trade-off? (3 points) (You trade off having something that provides exercise, allows you to be outside, and can be used with several friends in order to have something you can play all year and which won't cause injuries.)

ACTIVITY 1: Answers (continued)

PRODUCTIVE WORKERS

1. A new computer can help employees do their work in half the time it takes without the computer. What economic concept does this illustrate? (1 point) (Increased productivity.)

2. New machinery can help a firm produce their products in half the time it takes without the machinery. How does this benefit the firm? Its employees? Stockholders? Consumers? Community? (**Note:** Could use different groups in different rounds of the game.) (3 points) (Enables employees to be more productive, improves return on investment for stockholders, lowers prices for consumers.)

3. The price of sugar goes up. How will sugar producers react? (3 points) (Quantity of sugar supplied will go up.)

4. The price of leather goes up. What will happen in the market for leather athletic shoes? (2 points) (Supply of leather athletic shoes will decrease.)

5. A firm can sell 2,000 basketballs at $15.00 each or 1,200 basketballs at $20.00 each. It costs $12.00 to make each ball. At which price will the firm make the most profit? (4 points) $20.00)

6. Pierre wants to increase his profits at the bakery. Will increasing his prices on all products help him increase his profit? Explain your answer. (3 points) (No, because at higher prices the quantities demanded will fall. For some products, this will result in a decrease in revenue and profit will fall. For other products, revenues will rise and profit will rise.)

RESPONSIBLE CITIZENS

1. Why is flood control along a river an example of a public good? (2 points) (Because flood control exhibits the characteristics of shared consumption and nonexclusion.)

2. What are taxes? Name a type of tax your family pays. (2 points) (Required payments to government; answers will vary.)

3. Provide an example of a nondurable good that you purchase. (1 point) (Answers will vary.)

4. Consumer goods make up one component of gross domestic product. What is another component? (2 points) (Investment, government spending.)

5. When analyzing a policy it is important to consider the pros and cons of each option. What is another term for pros and cons? (3 points) (Benefits and costs.)

ACTIVITY 1: Answers (continued)

PRUDENT SAVER

1. What is interest? (1 point) (Payment for the use of money.)

GLOBAL PARTICIPANT

1. Even though orange trees will grow in the state of Illinois, farmers there choose to grow crops such as wheat, soybeans, and corn? Why? (2 points) (Comparative advantage.)

2. How does specialization and trade benefit consumers? (1 point) (More products available, lower prices.)

3. The U.S. government levies an excise tax on leather goods imported from other countries. What is the impact of this tax on U.S. consumers of leather goods? (3 points) (Fewer choices, prices rise.)

4. You are a sugar farmer in Central America. How do you feel about U.S. excise taxes on the sugar you ship to the U.S.? (5 points) (You are probably opposed to the tax. It makes your sugar more expensive than U.S. sugar. As a result, you sell less sugar.)

VISUAL 1
CIRCULAR FLOW DIAGRAM

Market for
Goods & Services

Families
and Individuals

Businesses

Resource
Market

GLOSSARY OF TERMS

capital resource   Capital resources are goods produced by people and used over and over again to produce other goods and services.

circular flow   The circular flow is a model that illustrates the overall operation of a market economy. Circular flow presents a highly simplified overview of how the economy operates. Owners of resources supply the services of their land, labor, and capital to business firms in exchange for money-income in the form of wages, salaries, rents, interest, and profits.

comparative advantage   The principle of comparative advantage states that a country will specialize in the production of goods in which it has a lower opportunity cost than other countries.

consumer spending   The purchase of consumer goods and services.

demand   The relationship between various prices and the quantities of a good or service consumers are willing and able to buy, during some time period, holding all other things constant.

durables   Consumer goods expected to last longer than three years.

economic system   An economic system is the collection of institutions, laws, activities, controlling values, and human motivations that collectively provide a framework for economic decision making.

entrepreneur   An entrepreneur is a person who assumes the risk of organizing other resources to produce goods and services.

exports   Exports are goods or services produced in one nation but sold to buyers in another nation.

final goods   Final goods are products that end up in the hands of consumers.

goods   Goods are things we can use, touch, and see.

gross domestic product (GDP)   Gross Domestic Product is the value, expressed in dollars, of all final goods and services produced in a year.

human resources   Human resources are people performing mental or physical work.

import   Imports are goods or services bought from sellers in another nation.

increase in productivity   An increase in productivity occurs when the same amount of an output can be produced with fewer inputs; more output can be produced with the same amount of inputs; or a combination of the two.

investment in capital goods   Investment in capital goods occurs when savings are used to increase the economy's productive capacity by financing the construction of new factories, machines, means of communication, and the like.

investment in human capital   Investment in human capital is an action taken to increase the productivity of workers. These actions can include improving skills and abilities, education, health, or mobility of workers.

market   Institutional arrangements that enable buyers and sellers to exchange goods and services.

natural resources   Natural resources are things that occur naturally in or on the earth.

nondurables   Nondurables are consumer goods expected to last less than three years.

nonprice determinants of demand   Nonprice determinants of demand are the factors that influence the amount consumers will purchase of a product at each possible price. The nonprice determinants of demand are the factors that can change the entire demand schedule and curve.

nonprice determinants of supply   Non-price determinants of supply are the factors that influence the amount a producer will supply of a product at each possible price. The non-price determinants of supply are the factors that can change the entire supply schedule and curve.

normal profit   Normal profit is the minimum payment an entrepreneur expects to receive to induce the entrepreneur to perform entrepreneurial functions.

opportunity cost   Opportunity cost is the highest forgone alternative.

GLOSSARY

productivity   Productivity is the amount of output per unit of input over a period of time.

price   Prices are the amounts of money that people pay in exchange for a unit of particular good or service.

profit   Profit is the return to a business enterprise that results when the value of sales exceeds the cost of the goods or services sold.

public good   A public good is a product or service producers cannot withhold from consumers who refuse to pay (nonexclusion), and the consumption of the product or service by one person does not reduce its usefulness to others (shared consumption).

quantity demanded   Quantity demanded is the amount of a product consumers will purchase at a specific price.

quantity supplied   Quantity supplied is the amount of a product producers will produce and sell at a specific price.

revenue   Revenues are the receipts from the sale of goods and services.

saving   Saving occurs when individuals, businesses, and the economy as a whole do not consume all of current income (or output).

services)   Services are activities people perform for others.

specialization   Specialization occurs when an economic unit produces a narrower range of goods and services than it consumes.

supply   Supply is the relationship between various prices and the quantities producers are willing to produce and sell during some time period, holding other things constant.

tariff   A tariff is a tax on an imported good.

taxes   Taxes are required payments by government.

BIBLIOGRAPHY

Aaseng, Nathan. *American Profiles: Twentieth Century Inventions*. New York: Facts on File, 1991.

Caney, Steven. *Invention Book*. New York: Workman, 1985.

Grove, Vicki. *Good-Bye My Wishing Star*. New York: Scholastic, 1989.

Haver, Louis. *Black Pioneers of Science and Invention*. San Diego: Harcourt Brace Jovanovich, 1992.

Hunt, Irene. *No Promises in the Wind*. New York: Berkeley, 1986.

Lawson, Robert. *The Great Wheel*. New York: Walker, 1985.

Lehrman, Robert. *The Store that Mama Built*. New York: Macmillan, 1992.

Lomask, Milton. *Invention and Technology: Great Lives*. New York: Scribners, 1991.

McClosky, Robert. *Homer Price (The Doughnuts)*. New York: Scholastic,

Mitchell, Barbara. *A Pocketful of Goobers: A Story about George Washington Carver*.

Montgomery, Elizabeth Rider. *The Story Behind Great Inventions*. New York: Dodd, Mead, 1953.

National Council on Economic Education. *Entrepreneurship in the U.S. Economy*. New York: National Council on Economic Education, 1994

_____. *The International News Journal, Inc*. New York: National Council on Economic Education, 1992.

_____. *Master Curriculum Guide in Economics, Teaching Strategies: International Trade*. New York: National Council on Economic Education, 1988.

National Council on Economic Education, Agency for Instructional Technology, and the Internal Revenue Service. *Taxes in U.S. History*. New York: National Council on Economic Education, Agency for Instructional Technology, and the Internal Revenue Service, 1992.

Rawls, Wilson. *Where the Red Fern Grows*. New York: Bantam, 1974.

Ware, Ethlie Ann and Greg Ptacek. *Women Inventors and Their Discoveries*.: Oliver Press, 1993.

Yates, Elizabeth. *Mountain Born*. New York: Walker, 1993.